HOW I MADE
A MILLION
TELLING THE TRUTH
ON YOUTUBE

HOW I MADE
A MILLION
TELLING THE TRUTH
ON YOUTUBE

Mike Quist

I dedicate this book to
our amazing YouTube Subscribers

TABLE OF CONTENTS

INTRODUCTION

WHY I WROTE THIS BOOK

When I sat down to write this book, I didn't have any great aspirations of making a lot of money or reaching the New York Times bestseller list. Instead, my goal with this book, from the very beginning, was to take everything I learned in my hands-on crash course with YouTube and beyond and put it down all in one place. My hope was that the hard-learned information in this book will help other people just starting out with YouTube find their way faster and easier than I did. A lot of people helped me along the way by imparting their knowledge, not to gain something for themselves but with the simple goal of helping another YouTube hopeful. This book is just one way that I hope to pay that kindness forward.

We all start somewhere, and I didn't start out with any hopes of being YouTube famous. Instead I was a contractor who worked hard to develop a great product. My original goal was to teach people how to use the product I had created. I assumed it would only be relevant to contractors and other handy men like myself. I quickly realized the best way to impart my information was through YouTube, which was a task easier said than done. Yet, despite my initial trepidation and almost entire lack of knowledge in the area, I found success relatively quickly. This book is an opportunity to both share my own personal journey while also sharing the secrets that brought me to where I am today.

HOW TO USE THIS BOOK

I designed this book to be a quick and easy read, so for those of you just starting out on this journey, you can read it from cover to cover and gain the foundational knowledge to start a YouTube channel and promote your business. That isn't to say this book won't be of benefit to seasoned YouTubers. It can also be used as a quick reference guide for those who have already gotten started but want some advice here and there on specific topics. I suggest that even experienced YouTubers should take the time to read through the guide from beginning to end. As someone who has found success at YouTube, I am always amazed by what I still don't know and what others, even sometimes less experienced or less popular channels, can teach me.

At the end of each section I include action items that help summarize the chapter and get you started right away with practical hands on steps toward improving your channel. These can be used as a check list and quick refresher as you move through each chapter. This guide is not meant to just be read, it is meant to inspire action. The saying goes that nothing worth doing is easy, but I have tried to make it as easy as possible to make clear measurable changes that will move your channel in the right directions. For more resources and links to the products that I mention throughout the book, please visit my website: StoneCoatCountertops.com

PART ONE:
YOU AND YOUR BUSINESS

CHAPTER ONE

You've Got to Give to Get

Contradictory to the title of this book I never brag or boast about money or success, but folks tend to listen more intently when they get real numbers. We went from $0 to $1.2 million in sales during our first 12 months. This year, our second year as an ecommerce business, we will have made over $5 million in sales. We started with less than 200 YouTube subscribers before our first sale, and today we have over 150,000 and are gaining about 20,000 new subscribers per month. We knew nothing about YouTube, online business, or modern marketing. This book will detail the exact process we learned. Now that the numbers are out of the way let's get started. You Got This!

YOU NEED TO GIVE TO GET!

For so many YouTubers and business owners whose number one goal is making money, my first piece of advice, which forms the crux of my philosophy, doesn't always sit well. It seems contradictory to the end goal of a successful business and flies in the face of our modern corporate money grab culture. Nothing is free, right? Wrong.

Put simply, "you need to give to get" means that you should aspire to give away, what you reasonably can, for free. Yes, FREE! This drives customers to your products or services and builds customer loyalty. If you don't make it past this first chapter, which I strongly recommend you do, you are in luck because you have already learned the most important lesson I have to share.

When I first conceptualized the idea of making "how to videos" that featured my products, I envisioned that contractors would pay for an educational video series that taught them how to use my countertop epoxy and techniques on how to renew old countertop projects that they used on their own jobs. I set to work. I spent hours filming groups of videos focusing on single topics of products as a way of providing workshops remotely. The thinking was that anyone who bought my video series would be invited to purchase the epoxy. I had spent ten years researching and developing my techniques, knowledge and epoxies through trial and error. I wasn't about to simply give that away for free. Nor did I think it was worthwhile to sell my epoxies to customers who hadn't been properly trained.

Needless to say, my plan fell short of expectation. After two years of trying to convince contractors that they needed my video series, only one went on to make a purchase. My initial expectations versus the reality of what was turning out to be a dead-end venture threw me for a loop. I struggled with doubt, questioning if I should scrap the whole plan. I came close, a number of times, to giving up on the videos all together, but the fact remained that I *wanted* to share my knowledge. I was proud of my product and enthusiastic about the techniques, tips and tricks I could share, if only my customers would give the videos a chance. The video series were good, and it felt like a mistake to abandon the idea. I knew my products were the best if only I could convince folks to try them.

It turned out I had been thinking about my product, business and customer base too narrowly. I approached my videos the same way I approached my products, from the mind set of, I have to sell, sell, sell rather than, I have to give. As soon as I put the videos up for free, my product sales took off like a rocket.

The mind set I had held onto for two years while I tried to sell my videos, came from the strong belief in the value of what I had to share, and it was further encouraged by other companies I found giving only teasers before roping customers into signing up for something or purchasing the full video or product. So many videos out there will show three-quarters of the information, but the really valuable information is withheld until the viewer pays money. It is possible that you will get some "customers" to sign up for your mailing list, clicking the subscribe button or maybe even a few that drop a couple bucks on whatever you are selling by hooking them with a partial preview, but I have learned from experience that those customers aren't coming back. They aren't the active users who write reviews, engage on YouTube, read your monthly newsletter or most importantly, continue to buy your product. My point is don't be stingy with what you know.

This understanding and acceptance opened up endless possibilities, and from there I came up with my three principals of YouTube Success.

THREE PRINCIPALS OF YOUTUBE SUCCESS

1. Entertain

Your audience is filled with savvy content consumers who above all else will not hesitate to skip your video within the first few seconds if they don't like what they see. The harsh truth is that there are millions of channels out there all vying for the attention (and money) of the same users. Unlike when I was growing up, when we only had a certain number of worthwhile channels to flip through, and we couldn't record to a DVR or play back from on demand, and we had to settle more often than not for our second or third choice of TV shows filled with commercials, today there is more content on YouTube alone than any one person could consume in many life times. If you tried to watch every video on YouTube right now without any more videos being added, it is estimated it would take you 60,000 years.[1]

---

[1]   https://www.quora.com/How-long-would-it-take-to-watch-all-the-videos-on-YouTube

What does this mean for the videos you create? Make them entertaining. It isn't enough just to share information. No matter how amazing, earth shattering or ground breaking the information you are sharing is, people will only suffer through boring videos for so long. In fact, you only have a matter of seconds to grab their attention. In those few seconds they have decided if your video and sound quality is tolerable, if they think you have something valuable to share and if it is entertaining enough to watch.

2. Provide something useful

Entertainment value is key to bringing in an audience, but you won't keep them, or drive them to buy your products, with entertainment alone. You must provide something useful. We have all seen the videos that have great thumbnails, titles and descriptions only to click on them and find that it is recycled talking points borrowed from someone else or a video completely void of any real information. This method may artificial boost your view counter temporarily, but those viewers will quickly move on to a channel, product and business that provides what they are looking for.

By being stingy with your knowledge or misleading your viewers, you also run the risk of provoking the angry YouTube commentators. Scroll through almost any YouTube video, and you will see the cut throat, no holds bar, nasty underbelly of YouTube, in which viewers harshly dole out their critiques and gripes. Viewers don't owe you anything but have the potential to give or take their praise and scorn at will. Your audience will either be your best asset or your biggest liability. They alone have the power to make or break you. By providing something useful within your niche market, whatever that may be, you have the power to create a community. A community that will grow independently and give back to you, your company and your channel ten times more than you ever provided for them, no matter how much you gave away for free.

3. Give It Away without Expectation

When you are spending time, energy and money on your content to make it entertaining and provide something useful for free, your natural inclination may be to expect something in return. Don't. The theory behind the give it away without expectation principal is that you will always be satisfied with your sales if you expect nothing.

This principal requires a lot of will power. It is easy to say that you won't expect your viewers to rush over to your website and buy your products or services, but it is another thing to not fall into familiar patterns of disappointment and frustration when your top subscriber has never dropped even a single dollar on your company. Do whatever it takes to leave your expectations behind. Instead focus on sharing your knowledge, creating entertaining and highly useful content with the goal of genuinely helping your audience.

The expectations you have for your audience have a way of showing up in your videos, even if you thought you were hiding them well. We have all suffered through those videos that feel a little too desperate for our attention or that outright beg for our support. Your audience will quickly recognize the underlying agenda of your video if it is only geared toward gaining something from them. The expectations you have for the success of your videos or the actions your viewers will take are not a burden that should be placed on their shoulders.

As soon as your audience recognizes your ulterior motives, you have undermined the first two principals, and more importantly, you are no longer really giving anything away for free. You have subtly attached strings to your entertaining and useful information that will all but guarantee turning off your viewers. Few people are willing to give their time and attention to videos that feel devious or underhanded in their marketing message.

When I began putting my videos up on YouTube, I assumed no one would care. I had spent years trying to get someone to notice without success. The videos had been designed for customers who had already shelled out their cash, so they didn't contain any type of marketing expectations. Even as people started finding my videos, and my community grew, I held onto the idea that any success that came my way was just an added bonus of sharing what I knew. Want successes, aim for it, work for it, but never expect it.

***

Recently, one of my commenters on my videos called me, "The Bob Ross of countertops." This is possibly the greatest compliment I have ever received. It meant that, through hard work, I had found the perfect balance of entertainment, information and expectations to engage my audience and turn them into customers. Depending on the status of your YouTube channel now, these three principals may feel like pipe dreams. Don't worry. This book will take you through how to follow these principals and reach your goals.

MASSIVE ACTION STEP

	Yes	No
Does my audience need to pay, subscribe or click to get the information I promised?		
Are there explicit or implied expectations of my audience in my videos?		
Are my videos not entertaining?		
Do my videos provide nothing useful?		

If your answer to any of these questions is yes, then the first thing you need to do is examine how you can change that. The answers to these questions provide the building blocks to the identity of your channel. It may be tempting to skip this and jump ahead to where we talk about video techniques and drawing viewers to your channel, but none of that will matter if you have not taken the time to apply these ideas to your videos. Regardless of what your business is, brainstorm ways to provide your audience with something useful, entertain them and let go of your expectations.

CHAPTER TWO

Know Your Company

Before you begin, you have to know who you are as a company. Your company is defined by the content you provide, how you interact with customers and how you choose to grow. Remember even a personal brand is a company. Understanding each of these cornerstones provides the foundation for decisions you will have to make throughout your company's growth to success. You will be faced with countless cross roads and question marks that will shape how customers see you and what your company becomes. Arm yourself with a solid understanding of your goals, purpose and policies before you begin. You may not think you are a business or may not be building your channel as a business, but my success was found thinking this way.

Begin with a solid mission statement. A good mission statement is brief. No more than a few sentences, it clearly defines what your company is trying to accomplish and the principals that you stand for. For instance, my company's slogan is, "You Got This." We apply this mentality to everything, from customer service to daily roadblocks that we face. There is always a way! We empower the DIYer and contractor to learn and grow a business using our products and remind them at the end of every video as we sign off, until next time from Stone Coat Countertops, YOU GOT THIS!

Our slogan and the sentiment behind it are brief and to the point, but it speaks to my desire to create a genuine and honest community for builders, designers, artists, woodworkers and DIYers with an interest in epoxy countertops, flooring, resin art, and woodworking finishes.

If you cannot formulate a mission statement, then you are not ready to start making videos. My mission statement informs my content and how I interact with my community. Each of my videos supports my company philosophy and adds value to the community I have built.

Ask yourself, what is my goal? It isn't enough that your goal is to make money or become YouTube famous. What are you going to contribute? What will you provide? How will you provide it? Challenge yourself to examine your niche, find your purpose and define your company in clear and certain terms. If you don't do the leg work ahead of time to understand your company, then your viewers will demand it of you once you begin sharing your videos.

CONTENT IS KEY

Based on your mission statement, formulate a plan for video content. This should happen before you begin making a single video. Throwing out as many videos as possible and seeing which one's stick will lead to inconsistent growth. Regardless of your mission statement goal, success with the YouTube platform begins with loyal subscribers. Viewers subscribe to your channel because they value you and your content. If your videos are unpredictable, viewers will simply look elsewhere for a channel that more consistently meets their needs.

This doesn't mean that you will never explore other content areas related to your niche, but without a clearly defined identity, you may be tempted to chase trends or appease every commenter. If your content begins to shift away from the original purpose, you run the risk of alienating your loyal subscriber base. Your company must be able to withstand the fickle tastes of YouTube comments without losing your way or abandoning the core of who you are. Simply concentrate on making great stuff!

Once you have nailed down your content, figure out how it will be monetized. We will go over marketing in more detail in part two, but before you begin it is important to consider monetization of your videos with ads. Initially, I didn't monetize any of my videos. Once I gained a larger, loyal audience of repeat viewers, I added some monetization. Most viewers will not put up with the interruption of ads if the channel is new or they haven't become loyal subscribers yet. Could I monetize them better now? I am sure I could. I could easily interrupt my videos with advertisements or end each one on a cliff hanger forcing my viewers to pay for the big reveal, but that would piss off all my viewers who have come to know my channel as a source for free, valuable information.

CUSTOMER SERVICE

Once you have a solid understanding of your content, the next step is defining how you will manage customer service. I hate the term customer service because it sounds combative. I don't view customer service as a defense against angry, unsatisfied customers, instead, when I refer to customer service, I am talking about every interaction you or your team has with viewers whether they have made a purchase or not.

Engaging with your audience will determine how your audience participates within your community. When I first started, I made the decision to answer every comment. You don't have to respond to every comment, but if you aren't, you have to be able to answer, why not? What are the guidelines for responding to comments? Which comments get responses?

Even more vital than the YouTube comment section is how easily you allow your viewers to get in touch with you. Will you provide a link to your website? Your email addresses? How about your phone number?

From the get-go, I included my website and phone number on my videos, so people could reach out to me. Finding a direct phone number these days on YouTube or even company websites is getting more and more challenging. You have to jump through hoops to get a person on the phone to ask the simplest question. As a business just starting out, an easy to find phone number was indispensable.

Answering every phone call and responding to every comment took time, but you have to ask yourself, how badly do you want this? How hard are you willing to work? The answers to those questions will determine how much your community grows.

Without a phone number, I don't think my company would be where it is today. We convert countless sales because viewers who have seen us on YouTube pick up the phone to ask a question about something they have seen. We don't spend the call trying to sell. We maintain the same philosophy of helping them with whatever project they are working on, but they gain a sense of loyalty and appreciation for being able to reach the real person behind the video. That cannot be replicated through videos and comments alone.

THE WORLD REVOLVES ON REVIEWS

If you follow the advice in this book, you are going to see a flood of positive comments on YouTube as people clamor to show their gratitude for the content you are providing. Positive YouTube comments are an important aspect of building your community, however they are not enough. Negative comments can be easily deleted, making even the positive comments untrustworthy for savvy customers looking for unbiased reviews. I never delete any comments, and I suggest you don't either, but it is important to have a third-party review system that users can trust.

Once you have set up your third-party review system, you need to gently guide people toward leaving reviews. Most likely they won't seek it out themselves, but every time someone leaves a positive comment, ask them to put it in a review. The third-party review system helps build a community outside of YouTube that can bring more people to your videos and website who wouldn't find you otherwise.

When my customers call and ask me for something, whether it is advice or a discount, I always try my best to give it to them, but I am always sure to follow it up with a polite request for a review. I guide them to my third-party site because they won't typically seek it out on their own. More often than not they are happy to provide a review. It costs them nothing, and it gives them a way to repay us for all of the free info and helpful hints we have given to them. Don't expect a review but always ask.

BUILDING YOUR TEAM

I did not grow my team until I absolutely had to. It may be tempting to delegate tasks out quickly as you find yourself working more hours with your attention on countless ends of the business, but no one is ever going to work as hard as you will to represent your vision.

I spent many years by myself working hard to learn everything I could about my niche, making videos, marketing, business practices, finances and everything else I came up against, so that I could personally oversee every aspect of my budding company. I wanted to be able to expertly handle anything that came up, so I wasn't dependent on anyone else to provide the services I needed or answer the questions my customers had. This was so tough!

When I had learned everything I needed to learn, so I thought, and my company was growing steadily, it was finally time to grow. My goal in building a team centered around my approach to customer service. I needed a team who loved my products as much as I did and believed that the best way to build a company was to help the community.

Everyone who works for me loves what they do. If they didn't, that would mean I was doing something wrong. I train each newcomer personally with the philosophy of the company as the foundation for how we interact with customers. We build our company culture on this.

MASSIVE ACTION STEP

1. Write a mission statement:

    a. _____

    _____

    b. (Remember: mission statements should be brief, concise and actionable. Other people reading your mission statement should be able to quickly get a sense of the purpose and philosophy behind your business or channel.)

2. Set up a third-party review account (google reviews)

    a. Be sure to link to it from your website and videos

3. We discussed the importance of learning things yourself. Fill in the table with the top five areas that you want to learn about and at least one resource where you can begin (keep in mind StoneCoatCounterTops.com has a list of all the recourses that I have used)

Topic to Learn	Resource
1.	
2.	
3.	
4.	
5.	

CHAPTER THREE

Don't Be Afraid to Start

Already, you may be feeling overwhelmed by the prospect of throwing your hat into the ring with the well-established and overwhelming number of YouTube channels that currently exist. YouTube has not released exact numbers on how many channels they have, but it is estimated that there are 1/3 the number of YouTube channels as there are people in the world. That equates to about one billion channels! And with 300 HOURS of video being uploaded every MINUTE, you are right to have some trepidation[2].

---

[2] https://expandedramblings.com/index.php/youtube-statistics/?cn-reloaded=1

DON'T BE AFRAID TO START

Start today. Don't let the fear of failure or the need to be perfect from day one prevents you from reaching your potential. Punch fear and perfectionism in the face.

When I first began down the path of making videos, I knew nothing. I didn't even know what I didn't know. I didn't know enough to be afraid. When it came time to put my videos on YouTube, I put them up without hesitation and without expectation because I assumed no one would care. For two years, no one had purchased them, so I imagined the response would be about the same for the videos out on YouTube, but I still clicked upload.

When my YouTube community started to build slowly over time, I realized that people cared because the content was really good. People couldn't believe what I was giving away for free, yet the video quality left a lot to be desired, if the comments were to be believed. I made it my life's work to learn everything I could. It became my obsession to assimilate the vast wealth of information about video production, lighting, editing, sound etc.

Mark Cuban, a businessman and investor, has said, "If you don't know more about what you are doing or the industry you are in than anyone else you are competing against, then you are going to get your butt kicked." I took this message to heart as a guiding principal for this new path I was about to take.

Looking back, I should have been terrified to start. I should have been filled with doubts of failure and missteps, but I am thankful that

I wasn't. Otherwise, I would still be trying to sell my low-quality video series without any success. Imagine if every time you had to drive to work you had to wait for every single light along your route to turn green, signaling that you wouldn't hit any setbacks or have to reroute or get slowed by delays. Wouldn't it be wonderful to know that you path forward would be smooth and successful? Yet, waiting for this guaranteed clear path across town, in the end, would only guarantee that you never left your driveway. Instead, it is better to begin right away, no matter where you are, what your path ahead may look like, or what questions are looming in your mind.

You will face setbacks. Accept that your first fifty to one hundred videos are going to be garbage. I shot my first video in my living room with one camera, no microphone and bad lighting. Over time, I learned how to make the minimal equipment and space I had work better. Then I learned how to upgrade to better equipment. You are going to get better with every video, every comment, and every effort you make.

That anxiety you feel is healthy as long as you put it to good use. There is no perfect starting line. There is no magical date on the calendar. If you don't start now, there will always be more excuses, more things to learn, more reasons not to start. Keep the reasons you wanted to start in the front of your mind and get going.

The starting line is just the beginning. Once you start, the possibilities open up, as long as you continue to learn, progress and build upon every success and rectify every failure. Strive to be the best, and then make it happen.

MASSIVE ACTION STEP

1. Create a list of reasons you started your YouTube channel.

   a. _____

   b. _____

   c. _____

   d. _____

   e. _____

2. Write down your first five videos that you will make after finishing this book.

   a. _____

   b. _____

   c. _____

   d. _____

   e. _____

PART TWO: MARKETING

CHAPTER FOUR

Website Overnight

Now that you have a sense of the purpose, goals and philosophies of your business, it is time to dig into the nitty-gritty of what makes a YouTube channel successful. The advice and ideas in this part of the book are designed to be instantly actionable. You can read a chapter and follow the steps right away to start down the path toward success, but again, I cannot stress enough how important it is to understand your business first.

That being said, before you can delve into marketing the first thing you need is a well-designed website. A YouTube channel is not enough. Regardless of what your business is providing, whether it is services, products or information. Your website acts as a home base for customers looking for more information or to make a purchase. Remember YouTube owns YouTube while you own your website.

When I ran a construction business for many years, I maintained a basic website that showcased my work to clients. The website wasn't much to look at and certainly wasn't geared toward driving sales. I used the original videos I made to show off the end product of my projects without giving away the steps to get there because I wanted my clients to hire me or pay for the full video series, but when I started giving them away for free on YouTube, I knew it was time to revamp my website. If a customer found me on YouTube and wanted to buy my products, I needed a way to offer it to them.

So, one weekend while my wife was away, I spent the evenings after the kids were in bed overhauling the website. I am in no way a computer engineer, well versed in code, luckily, now a days, with website builders like Wix.com, Squarespace and Godaddy, anyone can make a do-it-yourself website. I am a big proponent of do-it-yourself, as most people who watch my YouTube videos can already guess. When it comes to websites, DIY has a few key benefits:

- o **Save Money**

  Paying an outside company to create a website, no matter how basic, can run you hundreds, if not thousands, of dollars. Cut and paste website builders are either free or have low monthly costs.

o **Stay in Control**

Rather than trying to convey your specific needs to someone who doesn't know your business, you have the opportunity to present a unique and authentic vision of your company in a way that only you know how to do.

o **Keep it Current**

Keeping your website updated with your latest videos, projects and product offerings is key to visibility on search engines and keeping your audience engaged. It is much easier to update your website, adding videos and content, if you have access, know how, and don't have to go through a third party and wait for them to fit your updates into their schedule. A consistently static website means there is no reason for people to come back and check out what is new.

KEEP IT SIMPLE

The key to an effective website is keeping it simple. The last thing you want to do after your YouTube audience has finally made the leap to clicking on your website link, is overwhelm or confuse them.

As you begin designing your online space, always follow the KISS principal, Keep It Simple, Stupid. Don't assume that your customer base is stupid but assume they don't know what you know about your industry. Make it simple for them to find exactly what they are looking for as quickly as possible. According to the Neilson Norman Group, the typical Internet user will stay on a page for only

59 seconds before clicking away.[3] These first few seconds are critical in the decision-making process of your customers. Bringing them from YouTube to your website platform is only the first step. The quality of your website will determine if they stick around for the second step of committing to a purchase.

Too many novice website builders worry about missing some tidbit of information that will be just the right thing for just the right customer and end up filling their page with paragraphs of information or links to countless pages delineating all the ways you are awesome. Consider your own browsing habits. How often do you land on a new website and click through all the pages or read every word on the page? If you are like almost everyone else the answer to that question is probably, rarely. The web has become synonymous with quick, easy information.

My website only provides four choices: Products, Gallery, Free Videos, and DIY recipes. These four categories represent the basic needs of anyone coming to my website. They are either coming to learn more, looking to see what can be done with my products or buying something. They aren't coming to learn the history of epoxy or how I got my start. Put yourself in the shoes of your potential customers. What are they looking for from your website and how are you going to provide it?

Too much information means they are wandering the page aimlessly. Design your page to draw the user's eyes to where you want

---

[3] https://www.nngroup.com/articles/how-long-do-users-stay-on-web-pages/

them to look. Consider what you want your audience to do when they land on your page and build your site around that.

MORE FREE STUFF

In keeping with designing your page around what your clients most want to see, give them more free stuff. Designing your page around what you hope to achieve helps streamline information and guide the user toward the most relevant areas but steer clear of bombarding your visitors with purchasing prompts. The bottom line is that we all want our customers to go to our site to buy something, but no matter how frequently we point them to our on-line store, they will make the decision to purchase independently. A heavy-handed approach to promoting your store is more likely to turn off customers than result in a sale.

When visitors reach my page, there are three key links that bring them to more free stuff as opposed to only one that asks for money. I give them more information on how to use my products, pictures of project ideas and finished customer projects and of course, links that will bring them back to my videos. Creating a one stop resource for everything related to your niche industry means they will have reason to come back over and over again and build brand recognition and loyalty.

As part of the drive to create a resource, my site has multiple ways to get in contact with me on each page. It is important to help customers feel like they have access to you and are part of your community. If they have questions before making a purchase, don't make them search through multiple other pages before they figure out how to ask that question. Everything should be easy and straight forward. I apply the same philosophies that provide the basis of my YouTube channel to my website function and design: provide something useful, give it away for free and keep it entertaining. In addition to those I keep it simple and give them easy access to me and my team.

DABBLING IN MARKETING

Your website is the first step of your marketing endeavor. Without it, there is no goal to your marketing campaigns aside from more video views. Once your website is polished and published, you can start down the path of on-line marketing. The world of advertising is complex and can easily become overwhelming. Start slowly. The next few chapters will delve into all the ins and outs, do's and don'ts of advertising.

MASSIVE ACTION STEPS

1. Make an account with website building software

2. Make a list of the four biggest reasons that your audience would visit your website:

    a. _____

    b. _____

    c. _____

    d. _____

3. Turn those reasons into page headings:

    a. _____

    b. _____

    c. _____

    d. _____

Get started on your website with these page headings as your foundation. Remember on the most basic level your audience needs to know how to contact you, how to make a purchase and how to learn more (not about your life story but about what you can do for them). Keep it simple!

CHAPTER FIVE

Jump Start with Google Ads

Once your website is up and running it is time to start thinking about advertising. It is easy to get lost in the complex world of on-line advertising. There are a number of factors to consider when creating a marketing campaign including how much to spend, what videos to share, keywords to use and the list goes on. Often as soon as you think you have a handle on your on-line advertising campaign all of the rules change. You will not master your marketing campaign overnight, or after reading a few chapters in a single book.

Don't get overwhelmed. Just like with every other piece of advice in this book, take it one step at a time. Use this chapter as a primer that can help launch your efforts while you take the time to learn more from every possible resource available to you (of which there are plenty).

MONETIZATION VS. ADVERTISING

Earlier in the book, I mentioned monetization. It is important to delineate the difference between monetization versus advertising. The two terms do not refer to the same thing and are both utilized to very different ends. Monetization is the process of allowing other YouTube channel videos to play before, during or after your own videos. When viewers watch the ad, you get a percentage of profits that Google makes for running the ad.

Advertising on the other hand is paying for one of your videos to play during other people's videos. This involves understanding your audience, key words, algorithms and analytics. Monetization helps you make a little money. Advertising improves your reach and broadens your audience.

WHEN TO MONETIZE

A lot of fresh-faced YouTubers, in their quest to make it big, get noticed or earn some quick cash, make the mistake of monetizing their videos as soon as they are eligible. While you may end up making a few bucks, you risk losing the hopes for a loyal audience, and you may be providing a platform for your competition.

Few YouTube success stories come from monetization. Nearly every well-known and profitable YouTube channel relies on a multiple revenue stream approach. If you want to make a million on YouTube, you have to use it for what it is-a far reaching platform to help build awareness of your company and brand.

Be strategic in how you monetize your ads. When I first started, I didn't monetize at all. I wanted to grow my audience, and all too often, if a viewer doesn't know the quality of your video or the value of the information you are providing, they will click away rather than sit through the 30 seconds to finish watching. I also ran the risk of the advertiser's video pulling my audience away from me. If my competitors are showing on my channel, I need to be sure that my audience isn't going to switch over to their channel instead.

Once my audience knew me and trusted in the quality I provided, I began to slowly monetize my videos, but even then, I remained very picky about what I monetized. Monetization works best with binge worthy content. Often my subscribers will binge watch a series of videos to see different techniques or colors. When I see that happening, I turn on monetization because there is a pretty good chance that they will stick around for thirty seconds to watch an ad. When I am putting out new stuff or when I am trying to reach a new audience, I keep the monetization off, so my audience is free to enjoy my videos without distractions.

Monetization is a simple process. Once you have reached a large enough view count, YouTube will allow you to turn on monetization through their Ad Sense program. Ad sense allows you to be paid and choose which videos are being monetized.

If you are serious about making a million on YouTube, then your goal should always be growing the company. Monetization is part of this, but only if you use it well. I use the money I make from monetizing my videos and put it right back into my ads. Try not to view the money you make from monetizing your video as profit in the same way that selling your product or services are profit. It may be money made, but not money in your pocket, yet. It is money for your business that is best utilized on your advertising campaign.

PAID ADVERTISING

Paid advertising is one of the most valuable assets in your YouTube arsenal. YouTube is a massive platform designed for the sole and specific purpose of sharing user generated content. That means that small business and individuals have the power of a massive media machine that was once only reserved for corporate executives with a large marketing budget and a team of ad experts. In fact, your reach on YouTube through paid advertising has the potential to reach a much larger audience than those commercials you see on prime-time TV with a tiny fraction of the budget. I have even managed to reach audiences on par with the Super Bowl attendance. Those ad companies spend millions for a thirty second spot during the super bowl while I started out spending no more than ten bucks, but I have the advantage of picking the targeted audience I want my ad in front of. If my ad returns a profit I simply scale, or increase, the budget. Also, if your ad is awesome, folks will share it on other platforms and you'll gain even more free views because you've made people aware.

Ads on YouTube have a power that no other platform can currently boast. It is targeted, specific, flexible and has the largest audience you could possibly hope for. Advertising on YouTube through the use of Google Ad words has been invaluable to my company's growth. Without it, I don't think we could have grown so big, so quickly.

STARTING YOUR CAMPAIGN

Despite being a complicated process, starting an advertising campaign is only a few clicks away. It all begins with a Google Ads account. Once you have signed up, you can create a campaign. Google Ads, when linked to a YouTube account, allows you to choose a video, and through key word targeting, YouTube will play that video to selected audiences.

Once your account is set up, you will run through a variety of prompts. All I can tell you is what works for me. Each company and channel have different customer needs and goals that will make their campaign different.

The first question, what is your objective, asks you to choose a goal of either: leads, website traffic, product and brand consideration and brand awareness. Again, each company has different needs, my overall goal with advertising was gaining video views, so I chose no goal. Since I am not trying to sell a well-known product that people will search for on their own, I need video views to teach them what I do before I lead them to my website. Driving people to my website or to sign up for a newsletter, won't help me in the long run if no one knows what the heck a countertop epoxy is or what they can do with it. My goal with advertising is to bring as much awareness as possible to people who have the potential to use my product given the right background information that they gain from my videos. In other words, I am trying to introduce people to my product. If you are selling a well-known product like baseball caps, then you don't need people to see your videos before knowing they need to buy your hat, so a different marketing goal may work better.

Once you have chosen a goal, you are brought to a page full of targeting information that helps Google and YouTube narrow your audience, so your ads only show to people that may have an interest. This is where it can become overwhelming. Questions like ad placement, topics and keywords can be both confusing and daunting. This is when you want to start seeking out every resource available. When you are first starting out, play around with your settings. Make multiple ad groups within the campaign, trying different settings, placements and targeting to see which ones have the biggest effect. Google has great customer service. If you call them, they will do their best to help you. Ask them what things mean and what might work best.

The success of your advertisement hinges on a lot of factors, the most important three are keywords, budget and video quality. Remember to start small and if the ad works you can scale the budget.

CHOOSING KEY WORDS

Unfortunately, I can't give you a list of ready-made keywords that will work universally. Keywords are specific to what you are trying to sell and the audience you are trying to reach.

Keep in mind that Keywords *narrow* your audience. An audience that is too broad or too narrow will not be effective. With an audience that is too broad, you will end up spending more money than necessary and reaching people who don't have an interest in your channel. On the other hand, if you add too many keywords, there may not be enough of an audience at all, shutting out potential new customers all together.

The best policy is to start with as few keywords as possible. This will give you the opportunity to narrow your audience when you start to see what is working and what isn't. I never would have guessed that woodworkers would be interested in my product, but when I started advertising, I could see through my analytics what keywords were popping up repeatedly. Woodworkers turned out to be a huge part of my business, and I was able to not only gear ads toward them, but valuable content as well. I should have known this group would love our stuff because I'm a woodworker myself and love to finish live edge slab tables with our clear finishes.

Start by making lists of words that relate to your product. Consider what you would search if you wanted to find similar videos. Also think about what words and phrases might lead to your video but aren't actually relevant. These are negative keywords and can be just as useful in filtering out users not interested in what you have to offer. For instance, if one of my keywords was DIY, I may want to remove words like cake design or crafts. While both of these are common in the do-it-yourself genre of YouTube videos, they don't apply to my content, so I tell Google, through negative keywords, not to play my ad for those group.

LET'S TALK MONEY

Google advertising through YouTube videos is a pay per click formula. Google will display your ads to relevant users based on your keywords. You won't pay Google anything if the viewer doesn't interact with your ad, but as soon as someone clicks on your video advertisement, or watches for a prescribed time, Google charges you.

It is up to you to determine how much you are willing to spend on your ad each day. This is your daily budget, and when you have reached your daily budget, Google will stop showing your ad. You can also specify how much you are willing to pay per click. Typically, you will choose a maximum bid. Essentially, you are competing against other YouTube advertisers to show your ad. When other people have a higher bid than you, their ad will be shown more often or more prominently. That does not mean you want to always be the highest bidder. That would mean your daily budget would max out more quickly and you may end up getting more clicks than you need if you are always the highest bid. How much you bid is not the only factor that Google considers. They also consider the quality of your advertisement as it compares to the keywords you are using.

I never paid more in advertising then I made in sales. This goal should be your guiding principal when deciding a budget for advertising. In the business world we call this *Return on Investment.* Return on investment means how much money you are making in return for how much money you are spending on your business. If you are putting more money into your advertising than you are making in product sales, then your business will not be able to grow. You will dig yourself into a financial hole that you may not be able to get out of.

What does this mean for your advertising? It means to start small. You can always increase your spending as your ads become profitable, but until you have worked out all the kinks of your ad, it is important not to waste money. The first time I turned on an ad, my budget was $10. Within a week, on only that $10, I got a sale for $300. That is a 30:1 ration. For every dollar I spent during that first week, I earned $30 in return. That is a nearly unheard-of return on investment ratio. That is the amazing thing about YouTube at this moment. As Gary Vee calls it, YouTube is underpriced attention. It may not stay that way forever, but right now, you have the opportunity to spend very little and get a huge return.

A 3:1 return on investment ratio is a reasonable starting goal, in other words for everyone dollar you spend, you earn three in return. A 10:1 ratio is a better long-term goal, anything above that means you have found sure fire success. Even if your return isn't quite that high, your initial goal should be to turn a profit. Know what money is coming into your business and what money is going out. How much can you spend to break even? How much can you spend to make a profit? We also consider all costs of doing business. A healthy ROI means your video content will grow your business.

As you discover what keywords work and what videos make the most impact, your sales will grow and so should your marketing budget. Just remember that your marketing budget should always remain lower than your profits. If you are selling a souped-up car for $100,000 your overall budget and average bids are going to be different than someone who is selling Made in China toys for five dollars each.

Like everything else in the online advertising world, your budget will depend on your needs. Stick to a low budget and get your keywords, your video and your bids right before you start spending more money.

WHAT VIDEOS WORK AS ADVERTISEMENTS?

A word of warning. Not all videos work well as advertisements. You shouldn't simply take your latest video, add some keywords and start throwing money at it to get it in front of people. Think about the kinds of ads that make you click on a link, subscribe to a channel or spend your money. Back when infomercials filled the late-night airwaves, Billy Mays and others captivated our attention with the big "wow factor," like cutting through a tin can with a knife and then slicing through a tomato, or spraying sealant on a screen door and turning it into a working canoe. If your advertisement is missing some sort of wow factor than it will not be effective.

I get that wow factor by piecing together the coolest parts of my videos on a given topic. I showcase the eye-catching 3D depth of our metallic finishes, pouring the epoxy, flashy color choices and the best finished products with some engaging music. All of it works together to pull people in within the first few seconds of my two-minute ad.

Keep your ad interesting, but don't forget to keep it on brand. If you don't know what on brand looks like for your videos than you better figure that out (more on this in Part Four). Each of your videos should have an easily recognizable common thread like logos, colors or music, so when they find themselves on your channel or on your site, they know they made it to the right place. Don't let yourself fade into the crowd or your advertisements will only end up helping your competitors. Showcase your best stuff, be honest, leave something to be desired and make it easy to find more.

When you are first starting out with advertising, you may only make one or two ads. As you become more comfortable with advertising, you will start creating more ads that may be more specific to different audiences. It is important to remember to match your keywords to your video. For example, I would not use "woodworking" as a keyword for a video advertisement focused on countertops. The obvious consequence is that when a user types in woodworking, but gets a countertop video, they won't click. Then google thinks my ad is no good and not relevant. So, if you have a few different videos that are each guided to a slightly different audience, make sure the video and keywords match.

***

Success in Google Ads is not about knowing everything. It is about finding what works for you. Get creative and don't be afraid to try different things. I made 1.2 million in my first year, but it didn't happen in the first month. It took all year of watching my ads carefully, tweaking the bids, budget, keywords, and videos. In January, I only earned $300, February over $3,000 by March I had generated $26,000 that month, by April I was up to $30,000 then by December my sales climbed to $240,000 in one month! After paying ourselves first, we took the profit we earned that first year and put it back into my business. I delved into every resource I could find. If I came across YouTube channels that provided valuable insight, I reached out to them, I asked them questions. Same thing with Google, I called them almost daily to get advice on my campaign. The knowledge to succeed is out there. It is up to you to find it and apply it to your own business.

MASSIVE ACTION STEPS

- ☐ Go to: www.ads.google.com/home

- ☐ Create a Google Ads account.

- ☐ Create a campaign

- ☐ Create a new "video campaign"

- ☐ Brainstorm a list of the five most relevant keywords

  - ▪ _____

  - ▪ _____

  - ▪ _____

  - ▪ _____

  - ▪ _____

- ☐ Choose or create the best video to use as your ad

CHAPTER SIX

Analytics, Algorithms and Where you Rank

Now that your Google Ad is set up and running, your video views and website clicks will hopefully start seeing an up-tick in visitors. However, running an advertisement and letting Google do its work isn't enough for the kinds of success we are aiming for in this book. In order to reach real commercial success with YouTube, your videos need to appear in organic search results too. Both YouTube and Google use algorithms to determine where each relevant video appears in the search results based on the value of its content. That may sound like a lot of nonsensical jargon, but in essence that means, based on how your video performs within certain criteria like watch time, subscriber, likes and user engagement, YouTube will show your video higher or lower in the search result lists when users type in relevant keywords. For instance, if a YouTube user types in the words "how to epoxy," those keywords may apply to countless videos, so YouTube has to decide which videos to show the user on the first page, second page and so on. That is where the algorithm comes in. It judges your video and gives it a ranking. This chapter is meant to give you a basic understanding of how to read your analytics and use them to improve your ranking in organic search results. YouTube Recommends our videos over 20 million times per month. For FREE. This is important.

ORGANIC VS. PAID

It is important to clarify the distinction between organic views versus paid views. Paid views refer to people who found your videos through your ad that is displayed on the top of the search results page or played in front of a video, because you are paying for preferential placement. Organic views refer to people who found your videos when they showed up naturally in either the search results or on the YouTube recommendation side bar. This chapter focuses almost entirely on organic rankings. While paid views are an important boost that help to get your videos in front of viewers right out of the gate, you shouldn't rely entirely on those ads to create a devoted fan base. Ranking up in search results naturally can help the performance of each consecutive video, improve the performance of your paid reach, and build a stronger community that ads alone cannot create.

The vast majority of my views come from organic searches. Even our best advertising can't possibly match the power of YouTube recommendations.

ANALYTICS

YouTube provides you with all of the information you need to be successful, all you have to do is figure out what it is trying to say. When you visit your "studio" you will see a link for analytics. Your analytics are all of the data that YouTube collects on your channel and how users interact with it.

YouTube tries to make things easy for us by placing the most important analytics most prominently on the page. You will see your watch time, views, average view duration, average percentage viewed, followed by likes, dislikes, comments, shares, videos in playlists and subscribers. The information is presented in a variety of ways depending on where you click. You can see it for each video, your channel as a whole, different time periods, and changes over time. It also shows you how your viewers found your videos whether it was through a YouTube search or an outside website.

All of this information can, admittedly, become overwhelming, but understanding it can mean the difference between your success or downfall as a YouTube channel. The following is a quick break down of what each analytic is and how it can be useful in better understanding how your channel is performing and how you can best improve it.

Analytic	Definition	What It Means
Watch Time	Total Estimated Minutes your viewers watched during a given time period.	This is the total time through all of your videos. The higher this number, the better your ranking will be.
Views	Total number of views within your selected filter and time period.	Helps you better understand where your views are coming from.
Average View Duration	Average minutes watched per view.	Understand how long people are watching any given video. If this number is too low it means that you brought them in, but the content of your video wasn't enough to keep them watching.
Average Percentage Viewed	The percentage of your videos that the average user views for.	If this percentage is low, you need to take a long hard look at your videos. Why are people clicking away before the video is over? At what point are they clicking away?

Likes, Dislikes, Comments	The breakdown of how many people have interacted with your video.	User engagement is a big part of YouTube algorithms, so the higher the likes and comments the better.
Subscribers	How many users subscribed to your video	Watch your competitors subscription count, know what is happening with them, so you can better understand your own channel and subscribers.
Traffic Sources	Tell you how viewers reached your video.	This helps you know your audience better. You can target content to those who already enjoy your audience while also trying to reach new audiences.

RANKING

YouTube uses these analytics to make their platform better. YouTube prides itself on being the second largest search engine, popular amongst a huge audience. Presumably, the execs at the top want to maintain their relevance, and they do this by knowing the value of their content. Just like you, they want their users to log more watch time. To do this, users have to be able to quickly and easily find content they are interested in. This is where suggestions and search results based on what people want to watch come in. Keywords alone are not enough to create useful search results. Just because something claims to be the single greatest video on DIY epoxy of all time doesn't meant that it actually is, so to solve the problem of false advertising and an overabundance of search hits, YouTube ranks videos based on their sophisticated algorithms to determine the value of videos based on the analytics they gather.

All of the analytics you see on your page are compiled by YouTube Algorithms that work to judge a video's relevance, value, and popularity. Videos with higher view counts, longer view times and more overall interactions end up higher on the organic search list. While it is impossible to know the exact formula of YouTube's algorithms, for instance, they may place different weight on different analytics, improving each analytic area becomes the key to improving your rank. Your goal should always be to get on the first page search results. Anything below the first page means that your visibility is very low.

A power tip, on our resources page we have a link to a chrome plugin called Vid IQ. This has been an invaluable tool to keywords, analytics, and different data that will boost your videos placement. Find it at https://www.stonecoatcountertops.com/

AUDIENCE RETENTION

Audience retention is an important key to ranking up in YouTube algorithms. Depending on the entertainment value, the information and the content will dictate how long folks consume your video and its message. Derral Eves, a world-famous YouTuber told me at a conference I attended that a 60% watch time was very good. Most of the information in this chapter will help improve your audience retention, from structuring your script, to titling your videos, to friction free tasks, but one of the most powerful ways to increase audience retention revolves around engaging with your audience. All of Part Three deals with how, when and why to engage with your audience. This is all about building your community through quick and meaningful engagement. The first twenty-four to forty-eight hours after your video is uploaded is the critical time for engaging with your audience. In fact, we now have a dedicated staff for this purpose alone.

SMART VIDEOS

It may sound obvious, but the subjects of your videos are an essential component to ranking high. Your goal when choosing video topics should be to entice new audiences to your channel while not straying too far from who you are. It isn't beneficial to stick to the same video topics every week, nor is it a good idea to create non-cohesive videos that don't relate to one another at all.

When choosing a new video topic for a standalone video or a video in a series, it is important to understand your market and your competition. Never make videos in a vacuum. Knowing what is popular and what your competition is up to gives you an edge to stay ahead of the trends. A while back, when the volcano in Hawaii was erupting, and everyone wanted to see the videos of the lava, I uploaded a video about an epoxy filled red metallic table called "Lava Table." I did not intentionally upload this video right when all eyes turned to lava, but as soon as I did, my view count took off. I had accidentally capitalized on a major trend. That isn't to say that you should throw popular keywords into your videos, instead you should know what is popular and how to apply it to your video niche.

So, how do you learn what is popular? You use the tool of the trade, YouTube. I start with the YouTube search engine. I begin typing in keywords related to my product. For instance, I might start with wood projects or woodworking and see what kinds of videos YouTube has determined are popular. I might find that farmhouse tables are a hot topic right now, so I can use that topic and apply it to my own niche, maybe making a video showing how to make a farmhouse table with our epoxy.

Research is the key to finding smart video topics. Use the search tool to find what is hot within your own market. Another strategy is to type in a keyword followed by underscore, a letter and a colon (I.e. epoxy_a:) this will bring up videos that contain the word epoxy and the letter a. This lets you do a more open-ended search, so you don't have to know exact keywords and phrases. There are times that I will go through the whole alphabet to find video ideas.

Another power tip is to use a plugin called Keywords everywhere. When you type in a key word it'll show you exactly how many people search that per month. I'll attach a link to this on our resources page at https://www.stonecoatcountertops.com

The simplest way to know what your audience wants to see next is to ask them. Somewhere within your videos, ask an interactive question to your audience. Ask if they like what you are showing them, if they want to see more or to suggest what else they would like to see. I learned about asking the "Question of the day" from Video Influencers, created by Benji Travis and Sean Cannell. This tactic is key to helping improve your video engagement, but it also provides you with valuable feedback.

When choosing smart video topics, it is important to pay attention to the YouTube community. You cannot be an inactive bystander and expect to come up with great content that everyone loves by happenstance. Do your research, know what people are talking about, know what people are watching, and know what YouTube is pointing people toward.

NICHE DOWN

Niching down goes hand in hand with choosing smart videos. I talk about niches all of the time. A niche is your small little corner of YouTube in which you can focus just on your own area of expertise. It is tempting to want to cover as much ground as possible, in an attempt to reach every potential user all at once. It goes, hopefully, without saying that this is not a beneficial tactic. When you are first starting out, the best thing to do is go as deep into your niche as you can.

If you are a DIYer like I am, then you know that is a huge and broad market filled with countless competing channels. The more specific you are with your content within the niche you represent, the more you will attract loyal users. The added benefit to going further within your niche, rather than broadening out, is that your competition will be significantly smaller. The number of users searching for DIY each day, I imagine, is probably an overwhelming number. We can easily assume that Do It Yourself receives more searches than Epoxy. While it may sound like a bad thing that fewer people are searching for your niche, that also means you know they want your content rather than landing on you accidentally. The same goes for every niche out there. The more specific you are to start the better chance you will have of ranking up. Once you have a solid foundation of videos within a small niche you can start branching out. If you start too big, you will never get noticed, and won't be able to rank up.

STRUCTURE YOUR SCRIPT

We will talk in more detail about your script and video production in Part Four, but what you need to understand, within the context of algorithms and rankings, is the structure of your script effects audience retention and therefore effects your rank. There are countless ways to structure a script, but whichever way you choose to structure your script, do it with purpose. Understand what works and what doesn't work. Below are the basic parts that any high-quality YouTube video should have at the bare minimum.

Hook

Hook them early with a quick glimpse of what you plan on showing them in the rest of the video. This part should be the flashy, wow-factor. I typically show some shots of the finished product and then will say something like, "Are you looking for a way to make your old countertop new? You are about to learn how in less than five minutes." Those two sentences engage the audience and then clearly, concisely and honestly explain what they are about to watch.

Branding

Next, we will show a 3.5 second clip of our logo and music while referring to our site address.

Delivery

Next, deliver what you just promised. Don't waste unnecessary time with self-promotion or excessive wordiness, get right into the valuable information of the video. Say as much as you need to get the message across and not one extra word, remember to smile two times bigger than normal.

Testimonials

I often include testimonials in one form or another to establish my authority and lend my videos some credibility. I will often show a screen shot of a review or go to an on-sight job with a customer. There are a number of ways to share testimonials, and you can get creative within your own niche. Remember people want reviews and in video form you can get very creative as to how brand trust is built, all while being 100% honest and transparent.

Outro

Lastly, create an outro. Thank viewers for watching, point them in the direction of more content, share the link to your website and ask them to like, subscribe and share. Spend a few moments explaining why you want them to share your video and how much you value their support. When your subscribers share your video, it has infinitely more value than if viewers find it through an ad. Shares become referrals that people can trust.

Analyzing the structure of your script can provide some pretty surprising insights when you compare it to your analytics. If your hook only last twenty seconds and your average view time for that video is twenty seconds, then you know, either your hook isn't strong enough, or your video topic isn't appealing to your audience. Spend some time watching what works and what doesn't work. When you have found the right formula for your videos and your audience then you don't have to hover over your analytics, but until then, you should be watching closely and comparing the results of each trial and error. To keep this simple always remember to MAKE GREAT STUFF! You make great stuff by simply getting better with each project.

TITLING YOUR VIDEOS

A few quick keys to titling your videos. When I first started out, when I saved my videos to my desk top after recording and editing them, I titled them things that would help me find them down the road, titles like "final cut blue table top." I learned that *file names matter.* The title of your saved video goes into YouTube's meta data. Match your saved file title to whatever you plan on titling your video for the YouTube audience.

When it comes to choosing a title, it is important to once again do your research before pressing upload. Think about what you type when searching for a video. Maybe you type in "How to teach my dog to sit." The top videos will match that search query word for word. This is not an accident. Don't get cute or fancy with your titles or no one will ever search it. Be honest with the users about what is in the video by titling it with exact words that you expect they would use to search. For example, if, in my video, I am turning laminate into a marble finish, I will title both my saved file and my YouTube video "Turn laminate into Marble DIY." My title is specific to the content in language that someone might use to search for that type of DIY project.

LONG TAIL KEYWORDS

Long tail keywords follow the same principles as titling your videos. To clarify, in the last chapter, we discussed keywords as they pertain to your Google Ads account, or keywords that, when searched, Google displays your ad. Long tail keywords refer to the keywords or "tags" that you add to both your video description and tags section when uploading your video.

Simply put, long tail keywords are keywords that consist of a string of words or entire phrases that more closely match the kinds of things users are typing into the search bar. Rather than adding individual words into my tags like *epoxy, DIY, countertops, laminate,* that may each apply to videos that have nothing to do with mine, I would turn them into one long tail keyword like "DIY epoxy countertops."

The phrase that you think your users would type in for the video you are uploading should be the raw file name of the video, the actual name of the video on YouTube, your long tail keyword and then it should be broken up and entered as individual keywords. Deciding what that phrase is, goes back to your research. What would you type in? What kind of videos appear when you use your own long tail keywords?

There are no hard and fast rules about how to develop your own long tail keywords. The important thing is that the keywords are honest and relevant. Tricking users into click because your title promises something you don't deliver is a sure way to have a short lived, flash in the pan channel with short overall view times. Your goal is to be in this for the long haul. That isn't possible without telling the truth.

REASONS TO BINGE WATCH AND FRICTION FREE TASKS

Users binge watch channels, first and foremost, because they find value in the content. This is where those first three philosophies come into play. If your content, provides value, entertains and gives it away for free, then you have binge worthy content. Yet, that doesn't automatically mean viewers *will* binge watch your stuff. YouTube's algorithms play a part here too. Every time someone watches one of your videos, YouTube provides suggestions in the side bar. If you are ranked high enough, and enough people have already followed up one of your videos with another one of your videos, then you have a good chance of showing up in that side bar.

You are not entirely powerless in the face of YouTube's algorithms. Aside from working your way up the ranking by following the rest of the advice in this chapter, there are three quick and easy options you can do right now to improve audience retention as far as watching videos consecutively in a single sitting. YouTube now allows channels to add end screens, annotations and cards to their videos.

End screens appear in the last twenty seconds of your video and allow you to add links to websites, videos of other content, other channels, and a subscribe button. If your goal is to keep viewers on your channel, then providing them with easy access to more content they will like is an invaluable tool to utilize each time you upload. As soon as the video ends, your users are presented with another video without the need to navigate through your channel or figure out what the next video in a series is.

When you are watching other people's videos, you may see little white dots pop up in the top right-hand corner that may say things like "watch now" or "learn more." These little info pop ups are called cards. When clicked on, these links bring your users to other videos or even your web site.   Cards, like end screens, are easy to add to your video. From your video edit screen in your creator's studio, simply click cards on the top bar and add a card. Cards can be as versatile as you want them to be. They can bring users to other videos or simply open a side panel within your video that shows related content, play lists, or polls. The benefit here is that if the user likes what they see, and either want more or want a video that is slightly different, in my case maybe a different color, they don't have to navigate away in order to find it. These tools are powerful to steer viewers to similar video content you suggest.

As with everything YouTube, there are countless resources on how best to utilize cards and end screens. Each tool provides their own benefits and potential drawbacks. The most obvious drawback of course is distracting from the content of your video. You don't want to bombard your users with pop-ups demanding they "click here." This runs the risk of breaking our three underlying philosophies if the user starts feeling like sitting through your self-promotion is the hidden cost of your content.

Think of cards and end screens as ways to help your user find the best content that is the most relevant to them. Experiment with what tool resonates the most with your viewers. There are no hard and fasts rules, so the best you can do is try each and watch your analytics as users interact with the different features.

I refer to these features as "Friction Free Tasks." Tasks that bring users right to where they want to go, and where you need them to go, without any extra effort. Our end goal, ultimately, is to funnel potential business to our website, but in order to do that, we want to build our audience, with likes, subscriptions, engagement, and binge watching. Make it as easy as possible for users to do all of these things.

When we were looking at our analytics, we noticed that a lot of older users, fifty plus, were watching our videos, but not subscribing. After some consideration, we determined this might be because at the end of our videos we were telling them to subscribe, but they didn't know how. So, at the end of our videos we added a quick how to, in which we simply showed a screen capture of how to subscribe and sign up for notifications. When we started doing that, our subscriptions jumped significantly.

MAKING A VIDEO VIRAL

A viral video is any video that becomes popular through sharing between one user to another. Like I have mentioned before, there is no greater compliment than a user sharing your video. That means they found value in it and thought others would too. Sunny Lenarduzzi, a prolific and knowledgeable YouTuber, who has provided me with countless advice, describes an acronym for how to make a video viral. Value-Intel or Info-Relationship-Authority-Leverage.

Value in your video, focuses on philosophy one, providing the user with great content. Value comes from what you are providing your viewers rather than simply trying to gain views for the sake of views, you are creating value within the community.

We have covered information already too. Sharing your knowledge with your audience should be automatically ingrained within your videos.

Relationship refers to how you engage with your audience both during your video and in your comments section. Use your video as a time to share information while talking directly to your audience. Be yourself, so viewers can get to know you. Ask questions that help your audience feel like they are an active participant. When you build that personal relationship, your viewers will feel a loyalty to your channel. We cover this in more detail in Part Three.

Authority is important, as I briefly mentioned before. How many times have you seen a video where you suspect the creator is simply making it up as they go along? Videos by people who appear to lack the authority of their subject, don't get shared. Demonstrate your experience while being honest and truthful about what you represent.

Leverage is the power to build upon past success to get more views for future videos. Our goal is to leverage the popularity of each video in order to encourage people to watch the subsequent videos. Once they have watched one video, get them to go somewhere else by leading them to your website or the next video.

UPLOAD FREQUENCY

It is important to let the YouTube Algorithm know that you are not sporadically posting random videos whenever you might get around to it. Channels that publish on a regular, frequent schedule tend to rank higher than those that post erratically or infrequently. If you can stick to a regular upload schedule whether that is the same day each week or every other week, then YouTube will move you up in the ranks automatically. This also helps your fan base get into the habit of looking for your new content on certain days of the week. Just like you might look forward to the latest episode of your favorite show, so you will tune to watch like clockwork. The same principal applies to YouTube viewership.

LEARNING FROM GREAT CHANNELS

This isn't the first time, nor will it be the last, that you hear me say, learn from your resources. Your greatest resource are other channels who are already succeeding at the YouTube game. Study them, ask them questions, engage with them, figure out what it is about their videos, thumbnails, and channels that appeal to you. Visit competitors, click on videos and sort them by most popular. What makes those videos popular? How can you improve on it?

Almost more importantly than watching your competitor's videos is reading the comments from their subscribers. What do their commenters like about their videos? What keeps them coming back? Also, what do their viewers complain or judge negatively about their videos? Are you making those same mistakes? In subsequent chapters we will discuss the power of feedback and the same applies to feedback your competitors get.

A few channels that I have found helpful are Sunny Lenarduzzi[4], Thinkmedia [5], Gary Vanerchuk[6], Darrel Eves[7], Roberto Blake, and Video Influencers. These YouTube channels revolve around helping other channels, like you and me, improve their videos and reach broader audiences. Whenever possible, as I grew and became more relevant to my niche, I reached out to them and asked for advice. Sometimes, they will ignore you, but other times when you get lucky, they will impart some knowledge and help you grow personally. Don't ever pass up an opportunity to learn, grow and build relationships.

MASSIVE ACTION STEP

1. Analyze your competition: Create a list of what videos, thumbnails, and search terms work the best? Why? Then think about what smart videos you can make (without copying directly)

---

[4] https://www.youtube.com/user/SunnyLenarduzzi
[5] https://www.youtube.com/user/THiNKmediaTV
[6] https://www.youtube.com/user/GaryVaynerchuk
[7] https://www.youtube.com/user/derraleves

Video, Thumbnail, Search Terms That Work	What Works About It?	Your Smart Video Ideas:	Longtail Keyword Ideas:

2. Use the following template to write a script (either write a new one or re-write an old one)

Hook:	
Delivery:	
Testimonials:	
Outro:	

3. Add your friction free tasks:

    ☐ Cards

    ☐ End Screen

    ☐ Subscription tutorial

CHAPTER SEVEN

Marketing Funnel

A marketing funnel, in essence, is your customer's journey with your product. Starting with how they are first introduced to your company and ending with where they finish in relation to your products. In other words, your marketing funnel is how customers are learning about you, researching you and ultimately deciding to do business with you. A marketing funnel, much like the funnel you would use to pour oil into a car is wider at the top and narrow at the bottom, a reverse pyramid. The goal is to catch as much attention at the top, using as many different resources available to you, in order to direct viewers down toward your end goal of buying a product.

When thinking about your marketing efforts, you have to work backwards. Consider what you want the last step or end goal of your funnel to be for customers. For my company, that last step is a purchase, but for other business models it may be committing to a service, buying a membership or any number of other actions performed by your customers. Regardless of where your funnel ends, think about the steps it would take for the customer who may be entirely unaware of your company, product or service to reach that final step. Each marketing funnel is going to be different, but each one should follow four basic steps: awareness, interest, evaluation, and commitment.

AWARENESS

Awareness is the first step of any funnel. This is when your clients are first coming into contact with you, your channel and your company. They may know very little about what you can provide. The goal of awareness is to let people know you exist and point them in the direction of where they can find out more. Think of it as the initial introduction.

Awareness happens in a number of different ways. Since this is the largest part of your funnel keep your options open for how to bring in new viewers. You can raise awareness for your brand, videos and products through your Google Ads, ranking up organically, other social media or any other relevant avenues that work for your specific company.

While your net at this stage should be wide, it shouldn't be so wide as to be obsolete, or you run the risk of making people aware who will never be interested in buying your product. This wouldn't be a problem except for the wasted time, energy and money put into the awareness step of the funnel to catch very few potential customers. Awareness is meaningless if you can't reach the right people. If my ad reached 100 people, but only two of them had any interest in DIY home projects, then my funnel would fail before it ever had a chance to begin.

The more you are able to target your awareness to people who are more likely to have an interest, the smaller the costs for awareness needs to be. Again, I think back to when I was young, and I watched TV during the summer when ads came on for local car dealerships or law firms or anything else geared toward adults, I would quickly flip past the channel. All the money those businesses threw at those ads missed a large percentage of the audience that saw them.

When companies didn't have the money for local or national ads, they would resort to cold calling. Neither of which are targeted or effective. A customer service rep could spend an entire day talking to a small handful of people none of whom might be the least bit interested in what you have to offer.

I think about my own company. Back in the days before YouTube took over the world, we found customers using home shows. Home shows used to be the route to getting in front of interested homeowners, in which contractors and companies would set up a booth at these large in person shows to try to convince people their product was right for them. If we had to resort to blanket ads, cold calls, and in person chance run-ins with an undetermined audience, our business would have folded before it got started. Building brand and product awareness should be as targeted and specific as possible. Home shows did work for us but when we discovered the amount of attention we could bring to our brand using YouTube, home shows went the way of the dinosaur in our marketing strategy.

Remember, regardless of your methods to raise awareness, you should always be guiding people to your YouTube channel as the next step of your funnel. It is unlikely a customer will jump right from awareness to the purchase, or commitment, step of the funnel. This may seem obvious, but it is important to have realistic expectations for your customer and your marketing funnel. Throwing one ad up on YouTube or Facebook isn't going to instantly lead to a flood of new customers. It will however trigger your marketing funnel.

If you make the mistake of leading them only to the link to make a purchase, you may be shooting yourself in the foot by not letting your funnel do its job. How many times have you seen an ad for something that caught your eye, only to click and be brought directly to a shopping cart. I can't speak for everyone, but I tend to quickly click away, so I can do more research. Few customers are ready to purchase after seeing a thirty second ad spot. They want to learn about the product and the company. They want to compare prices or read reviews or decide if the product is right for them at all. My customers will typically take *two weeks* from the time they are first made aware with the very first ad to when they go to the website and make a purchase. In that time, they are not simply sitting around quietly debating, they are interacting with my content, watching my channel and even asking questions. It is important to make sure your funnel is ready to provide them with that.

Social Media

We utilize almost every social media platform to widen our funnel, including: Facebook, Instagram, Pinterest, Twitter, Snapchat, Tumblr and anything else that comes into the social media lexicon. Everyone has their favorite, go to, platforms that they check regularly. Some potential customers may be on Facebook, but rarely go on YouTube, so relying only on YouTube is a mistake.

Each social media platform is unique in how it presents its content and reaches its users. That doesn't mean that we create brand new content for each page or rewrite how we do everything. Remember, that we only use the other social media pages for the *awareness* phase of our funnel, so our goal is to direct them back to YouTube.

We do this by segmenting the content that we have created for YouTube out for the other platforms. For instance, on Facebook, we found that if we embed a small clip of our latest video along with a link to YouTube, people will watch the embedded video and click the link, whereas when we simply link to YouTube videos, fewer people follow through to YouTube.

As you are experimenting with other social media, remember the purpose is only to increase awareness and bring them further into your funnel. Some companies use the other social media further along in their funnels either to inform or evaluate, but I have found that the other platforms are not well formatted for longer form videos in the same way YouTube is.

INTEREST

Once people have become aware of you, the goal is to give them more entertaining information to get and hold their interest. Maybe they followed a Facebook clip to YouTube or they saw your ad and want to see the full video, regardless of how they got there, the most important thing is to keep them there. During this phase, viewers and potential customers are deciding if you are worth their time-make sure that you are. Everything in this step is about keeping interest. You have already done a lot of the leg work for this when you took the steps delineated in the last chapter. The higher you rank, the better your content, and the longer viewers will maintain interest.

The biggest problem faced by companies, with both longer or shorter marketing funnels, is that customers will have an initial interest that fades before they move onto the next phase. They can get busy with the usual demands of life and forget about you before moving down the funnel. Marketing funnels that are longer, like mine, run into this problem because it takes a few weeks of watching how we make old nasty countertops look like new high-end natural stone before most DIY folks are convinced they can get similar results. My customers, in particular, want to make sure they have the skill set to take on a DIY project like the ones my products offer. Other marketing funnels may be shorter. They don't have to worry about the interest piece on the first round, but if their company relies on repeat sales, then they have to consider interest as customers are considering buying again. It doesn't matter the position your marketing funnel is in, the key is to maintain interest.

Beyond keeping them engaged with your videos and the community, consider ways that you can stay relevant and remind viewers about your company, products and channel. The first way to remain relevant is to publish videos on a regular schedule like we talked about in the previous chapter. Subscribers will then get notifications of your latest videos which will bring them back to your channel.

Publishing on YouTube is not the only way to stay in the minds of your viewers. Get creative with how you are reminding people but carefully avoid the mistake of giving too many reminders. Otherwise, your viewers may feel bombarded by "spam." There are many ways you can keep interest up including, polls, free or cheap samples, contests, e-mail lists and re-marketing.

A subscription-based email list is a great, gentle reminder. Your email list should be opt-in rather than required to access more information. Most importantly, the regular emails that you send should still follow the three main philosophies that your YouTube channel follows. They should be entertaining, informative and free.

EVALUATION

Evaluation goes one step beyond interest. Once they have developed an interest, most customers are going to spend some time, however long or brief that may be, evaluating the quality of your company and product in order to determine if it is right for them. Once again, YouTube is your greatest tool for evaluation. The more they watch your channel, the more time they are spending considering your product, eventually they start asking themselves questions. For my product, they are asking, "Can I see myself in my bathroom or kitchen doing that kind of work?" With a strong YouTube channel that allows them to browse everything you have to offer, they can get most of their questions answered. Your YouTube channel helps potential customers become part of the community before they have spent a single dollar. They get to know you, your product, how your company operates and more, simply by watching entertaining, informative videos.

Eventually, during the evaluation process, customers who are on the precipice of making a commitment will have more in-depth questions about how our products will work for their specific needs that may be difficult to answer on YouTube. This is where our high-quality customer service becomes so vitally important. We want to make it as easy as possible to find the answers. We don't want them to have to scroll through countless comments or search through all the videos we have uploaded to ask if they can put a hot pan on the counter they are thinking about making, or how much epoxy they will need for the island they are considering building.

Those final questions may be the last step in their evaluation process and could mean the difference between committing versus walking away. Evaluating your product should be the easiest thing viewers do. Point them to reviews, give them your phone number, respond to comments, make yourself available in any way you can. How many times have you read a "yelp" review of a restaurant that raved about the wonderful food but complained about the service ending with a one-star rating and a vow to never return. Service is an important part of the evaluation. It helps your potential clients see themselves crossing that final hurdle and becoming real clients. They want to know that if they take the plunge and buy your product that they won't be all alone in their kitchen with an epoxy that they don't know how to use or whatever the equivalent analogy for your business may be.

If you find that viewers are making it all the way through the funnel, to the point that they are watching multiple videos, subscribing, binge watching and joining the community comment section but not committing to a final product, then you may not be solving a big enough problem. We have spoken a lot about the huge reach that YouTube provides, but it is our job to use it to our advantage while still following our three philosophies. What is the "Pain point" of your audience. Our audience wants new fancy surfaces in their remodel project without the high costs of natural stone. During your videos you should be presenting a problem that you hold the keys to solving. This is just another subtle way to help your potential clients see themselves using our product. If the top of your funnel brought in the right people, then when they are in the evaluation step, they should be able to instantly relate to the problem you are solving. The artist that uses our epoxy has much more working time to create beautiful art than other fast setting resins that heat up. Woodworkers love our epoxy because it will lay out and the bubbles generated during the mixing process are easily removed as opposed to other products that leave their table finishes full of waves and bubbles. DIYers love our products because they actually get the amazing looks they see on the videos. Learn what pain point your product solves, tell the truth and watch your funnel do its job.

COMMITMENT

At Stone Coat Countertops, commitment means a purchase. Commitment may mean different things to different businesses, but in the simplest terms this is when a viewer turns into a customer. If you have done everything right in your marketing funnel up to this point, you will start seeing more viewers making commitments. By the end of your funnel, when viewers are on the verge of buying, if you haven't made it a no-brainer, then they aren't going to buy. More importantly that means there is something broken in your funnel. Somewhere along the line, your potential customers are trickling away to either other companies, other products or have given up on the idea that they need what you provide in their life all together.

The commitment step can become the most hands-off step. As long as you have a website that is user friendly and a support team ready to answer final questions, your customers have already made the decision to buy once they reach this step. That being said, re-read chapter four and make sure your website is up to the job of sealing the deal. If customers have made it all the way through your funnel, the last thing you want is for them to reach your website and get confused over price, shipping or how to order.

BEYOND COMMITMENT

When a customer makes a purchase, your marketing funnel may technically be over, but that doesn't mean you should call it quits. Consider each customer as a customer for life. Do this by following up on their purchase. Check-ins can be through an automated email or a more personalized communication, either way be sure to ask them if they enjoyed the product and gently guide them to where they can leave a review or share pictures of what they have done with it.

Gary Vee talks about providing more value than you are asking for. The ratio of what you give to what you get at the very least should be 51:49[8]. Meaning, you should be giving 51% for every 49% you get. I use this philosophy everywhere. Even with my own employees. I am constantly trying to give 51% while I am only asking for 49%. When I give my employees more than I get whether that is in terms of salary, support, vacation time, rewards, etc. They try to do the same for me and it becomes a contest of who can do more for the other. The end

---

[8] https://www.garyvaynerchuk.com/giving-without-expectation/

result is an amazing work environment in which everyone is happy and working hard for the wellbeing of each other and the company.

In terms of your customer, you don't ever want the customer, subscriber, or casual viewer to feel like they are getting *less* than what they put in. You never want a viewer to finish watching a video with the feeling that they wish they had that seven minutes of their life back. Equally as important, if they feel like they got a good deal for their money, they will keep coming back to buy more, or they will write a positive review. The counter example to that is a customer who feels like they got swindled out of their money will make that known to future customers.

The bigger you can tilt that scale at the end of the funnel means viewers will not only take the final step to commitment, but they will become repeat clients. That 51% means that your product out performs the customer's expectations and that your company does as well. Once they have made that purchase, don't abandon them, instead make them part of the "family" with an avenue for help, support and community as they use the product. A quick pro tip: name your subscribers. This sounds funny, but it works to build community. We call our subscribers "Insiders." When we address viewers in a video we say, "What's up Insiders?" Insiders explains to our community they are on the inside track to the tips, tricks, and tools of how to use our products to make great stuff.

FINAL TIPS

Understand Motivation

Understand the motivation of your clients. What are the reasons clients choose your product? Why choose your product or service versus another? For example, my customers tend to fall into three categories, 1. People who genuinely enjoy making things themselves. 2. People looking for a cheap solution. 3. Customers who need something done quickly. Those three reasons describe three very different customers. Understanding each one of them helps me better target my funnel each step of the way. I can spend time on each of my videos talking directly to one of those motivations. In order to better understand my buyers, I also have the option of making individual videos for each one: "Turn Old Formica counter tops into beautiful granite in under a day" versus "Don't waste your money on expensive granite." Then I can watch the data on how each of those performs.

Your Product and services

Make sure your product or service performs as advertised. Our funnel only works because our product does what we say it will do. You can have the best marketing funnel in the world, but if, when customers receive your product, they are disappointed, or it is misleading, then they will not come back, they will leave negative reviews, and they will turn away other customers.

MASSIVE ACTION STEP

1. Check that your funnel is in order:
   a. Awareness: YouTube Advertising & Social Media
      i. Create a business account for all of the relevant social media platforms.
      ii. Spend some time researching each platform to determine the best way to tweak your content to each platform. i.e. pictures for Instagram, video announcements on twitter, video clips on Facebook etc.
   b. Interest: YouTube videos
   c. Evaluation: YouTube & Helpful Available Customer Service
      i. Re-read Chapter Two and take a critical eye to your customer service practices.
         1. What is your response time?
         2. Are customers able to reach you easily?
         3. Are customers satisfied with the experience?
         4. How can you improve customer service?
   d. Commitment: Website
      i. Spend some time with your website. Try to see it from a customer's point of view.
         1. Is it easy to make purchases?
         2. What can you do to improve it?

e. Beyond Commitment: Follow up & Reviews & pictures

    i. Create a procedure for following up with your customers

    ii. Do customers know where to leave reviews or send pictures?

PART THREE: ENGAGING

CHAPTER EIGHT

Know Your Audience

We have talked about engagement a few times so far, most notably in Chapter Six; Analytics, Algorithms and Where you Rank. Undoubtedly, engaging with your audience is a vital component to ranking up in YouTube organic searches, but there is more to engaging than simply improving your visibility. The ways in which you engage with your audience will define your company and what you stand for in the minds of your audience just as much as your video content. Engaging also brings the opportunity of better understanding your audience, allowing you to make informed decisions about content. Knowing your audience is a win-win situation. You know your audience by engaging and you engage to know your audience better.

THE PARABLE OF RANDY COUTURE

Randy Couture is a World Champion UFC fighter. A buddy of mine, Scott Smith, was an amateur MMA fighter. He had a great career and eventually made it to the UFC, but before he did, he was fighting at a smaller venue. Randy Couture happened to show up and watched my buddy warming up. After a few minutes, he asked him if he could corner him during the fight. Of course, Scott was thrilled to have a World Champion coach him through a match. Scott ended up winning and maintained a great relationship with Randy. What is the point of all this, you ask? Randy Couture was successful and famous. He didn't need to show up at smaller venues. He didn't need to meet with his fans or up and coming fighters, but he did. He showed up to small venues, he brought posters, he personalized every signature. The result? My buddy Scott, along with countless other fans, never once missed another Randy Couture fight.

Never underestimate the power of knowing your audience and making connections. I tell all of my employees this story, so they can use it as a guide for how to view our own YouTube audience. Treat every subscriber and every commenter like gold. Assume that at any moment each of your subscribers could choose to turn away one by one. Work hard to know them, engage with them and make a personal connection with every available opportunity.

STUDY YOUR AUDIENCE

Effective engagement begins with studying your audience. Know who is watching, when and why. When we first started our YouTube channel, we didn't know much, if anything, about our audience. We simply made a video of whatever project I happened to be working on at the time. When I began studying my audience, initially through YouTube analytics, I learned that they were majority male. Given the nature of my business, I wasn't all together surprised by this, but I noticed an interesting trend. Whenever I brought my wife on to do a video with me, my female audience increased and moved closer in numbers of my male viewers. As I continued to experiment with this shift in audience demographics, I learned that most of the artists that follow my channel and using my products were female.

Similarly, when we geared videos toward woodworking, our views increase three-fold above that of our countertop videos. As I tested the theory with farmhouse tables or reclaimed wood, I better understood the interests of my audience, as I studied the demographics of views. In the previous chapter I mentioned a story about helping 55 and over viewers use the subscribe button, studying my audience was how I learned about that demographic.

I learned how diverse our viewership could be as well as the limits to that range. Through trial and error within the different demographics, I got a clear sense of who my audience was and why they were tuning into my channel. I could make video series geared to each demographic or try to hit each interest point in each video. I brought in my wife, my mother and female employees to help film videos to reach the female audience when doing more artistic projects. I made multi-video wood working series and made helpful hints for my less tech-savvy community members. Knowing my audience better helped me plan my videos and outline my content. Further, by knowing these specific demographic details about my audience, the comments they left started making more sense and gave me a foundation with which to engage.

LISTEN, TALK, ENGAGE, REPEAT

The demographics provided by YouTube are the first place to start to get to know your audience. You can see a clear break down of who is watching your videos and for how long, but don't stop there. Your audience will tell you everything you need to know when they leave a comment on your videos.

When I first started making videos, every time someone left a comment, it was a sign that they cared enough to take that time out of their day to leave feedback on my channel. I still consider every comment with just as much enthusiasm now, partly because I consider the philosophy of Randy Couture, but also because each comment meant something to the person leaving it, and in turn, gave me a glimpse into why they are watching, what they are gaining, and what else they are looking to learn. That isn't to say that all comments are kind and supportive. We will discuss in the next chapter how to handle these, but regardless of the sentiment, I viewed each comment as another form of analytics.

I knew my audience because I listened, I responded, and I encouraged more engagement. Each time I comment on a user's feedback, my goal is to encourage another engagement. Rather than simply saying thanks to a compliment, I say thanks and ask a follow up question. I have come to a place where I know what to say in order to keep my audience talking, but I didn't get there overnight. It took time getting to know my audience and committing my time to engaging them in real conversations that don't revolve around self-promotion, like so many other channels can fall into.

MAKE A GOAL AND SOLVE A PROBLEM.

Your audience should become the driving force of your channel. I learned that my audience spans, people looking to repair or cover laminate, woodworkers, artists, house flippers, people who own RVs or Yachts, contractors looking to improve their business, even entrepreneurs who see a massive opportunity. Each unique niche in our audience brings with it their own needs, interests and struggles when it comes to my videos and products.

Remember, you should always be giving more than you get, so when you are getting to know your audience it isn't just a scheme to rank up or manipulate them into engaging further. Studying your audience should be done from a place of genuine interest in helping them and bringing them into your community, thus using your videos to solve a problem. When I really started listening to my audience I got a sense of the individual problems they faced, each bringing a different angle to the work I was already doing, while trying to renovate or create a piece of art work. I spoke briefly last chapter about presenting a problem and solving it in each of your videos. You know what problems to solve by knowing your audience.

My audience's goals became my goals. I took the problems they struggled with and turned them into the goals of my videos. I made sure each video had a clear, specific goal that I stated up front. I asked myself who is this video for? What will they gain by the end?

To that end, I started including something free to give away in each video, in addition to simply providing information. This can be as simple as a PDF download on your website. For example, I found that my audience watched my videos until they were ready to buy, but then when they got to my website they became overwhelmed by the choices. They often wanted the exact colors and products they saw in my videos, so I created step by step checklists for all the tools they would need to complete the project they were watching. We set it up, so a card popped up on the screen offering the free PDF checklist. When customers clicked on it, they could type in their email and download the PDF. The email subscription is of course optional, otherwise it wouldn't be free, but in the first day we collected over seven-hundred emails.

The benefits of this can be many. First, you are helping your audience by giving them more. Second, you are driving your audience to your website. Third, you can see the direct impact each video has on website traffic and PDF downloads. Fourth, you are improving your marketing funnel, and finally, you are creating more opportunities for positive engagement. A pro tip here is by keeping the email list for each freebie you offer separate, you will know who to market to when you have future offers. You can also use the email list to have Google Ads market to similar interest. This is one of the most effective unlocks we have discovered. For example, if we are giving away a recipe for a specific art style we will name our audience artist. A countertop downloadable PDF check list will have an audience labeled countertops. Make sense?

COLLABORATE

The term engaging isn't exclusive to active members on your channel. Remember my story about Randy Couture? He didn't just engage with his fans. He engaged with his entire community. Collaboration is a huge part of being a relevant YouTube channel. A lot of support can come from those who are in this with you.

Recently, I flew down to Texas, armed with cameras and microphones to meet up with one of my amazing subscribers and fellow creator, a channel called Artist Till Death. They were a smaller channel of only about 13,700 at the time, but they had amassed such a devoted and highly engaged audience, that every night they did a live video of a new piece of art. Often, they had used my products in their videos and they made some really amazing stuff, so I decided it was time to meet them in person for a collaboration. I wanted to help support their channel because they had already guided so many of their subscribers over to me, just by showcasing my products.

After our two-day collaboration, my subscribers and product purchases sky rocketed, and their subscribers boomed as well. While recording together, I provided their audience with a unique coupon code, so I could track how many of their subscribers actually made the transition into real customers. More than I had initially anticipated used the code to purchase from my website after the live feed. Despite being a smaller channel, their devoted and highly engaged fan base "The ATD Fam" joined my community, creating a larger mutual community between the two of us. Gaining more customers wasn't the only reason I collaborated, it certainly was an added plus, but the greatest thing I gained was a long-term mutually beneficial relationship with another YouTube channel.

AUTHENTICITY

All the way back in Part One, I talked about knowing yourself. Part of the reason that we need to know our audience is because it helps you better define yourself. Your audience has gotten to know you through the videos you have uploaded. It is important not to stray too far too quickly from the crux of this identity.

While I was doing my homework and watching a competitor of ours, I quickly realized the host felt like a sales man. They had some good content and they seemed to know what they were doing, but the host had fancy business man clothes on to work with epoxy. When I scrolled to the comments, I realized I wasn't the only one who had noticed. None of the viewers could appreciate the content the channel was putting out because they were so distracted by what felt like an inauthentic persona to them.

When I was younger, I sold security systems door to do, and my father gave me a motivational twelve tape sales course by Tom Hopkins that focused on how to sell effectively. Tom would say, in his tapes, to act like a lamb and sell like a lion. In other words, the goal is to be unassuming. You don't want a contrived persona to overpower what you are trying to sell. If I tried to act like a big shot instead of a construction guy with a lot of useful knowledge to share, no one would have connected with me. Remember first, you have to be the person with the real experience you claim. You need to tell the truth.

You don't have to, nor should you, stay the same forever. Most channels grow and evolve naturally over time. The point is not to force a change to the point of alienating your viewers. Just because my channel is growing, I am meeting cool people, and getting publicity, doesn't mean I need to change myself. I still wear my Stone Coat t-shirt and get messy. I do however continue to grow. I constantly try to improve my videos, my connections, my content, my website and my customer services. My videos look very different than when I first started out, but my company and channel have stayed true to who I am and my three philosophies. Get better but don't change who you are.

MASSIVE ACTION STEP

1. Study your audience:

    A. Look at your demographics. Track how your demographics change with each video. Why? What can you do to bring more of the demographics to each video?

2. Listen and respond

    A. Listen to what your audience says. What kinds of questions are they asking? What kinds of problems are they facing? What is their biggest concern or greatest compliment?

    B. Use the comments to inform your responses to get them to engage more.

3. Read through the comments on a few videos. Create a list of problems to solve.

    A. What video topics could help solve these problems?

    B. Make a list of video goals from the topic list.

4. Go through your subscribers and frequently active viewers. Make a note of which ones are other channels. Make a point of reaching out, thank them for their subscription, engage on their channel. Once you have spent some time getting to know them decide if a collaboration would be mutual beneficial.

CHAPTER NINE

Taping into the Power of Feedback

Like we explored in the last chapter, the comment section of your YouTube channel can give you more valuable insights than any other form of analytics, so long as you use it correctly. Feedback becomes a crucial avenue for getting to know your audience, ranking higher in organic searches, developing trust, and learning valuable lessons about your channel.

HOW TO USE NEGATIVE FEEDBACK

I start with the power of negative feedback because it is actually more useful than praise, and it is so much easier to overlook. Negative feedback often feels like a personal attack. People show up to your channel and all they have to say is what they hate about you or your video. It is a natural first instinct to bristle and jump into defensive mode, but you have to fight against that quick reaction. Otherwise, if you jump to defend yourself, you run the risk of alienating not only tentative viewers who have left the negative comments, but also other viewers who will be turned off by the negativity on your page.

When I first started out, one viewer, who was a really direct, no nonsense type person, commented on my video about how awful my sound and video quality were. My first reaction was to get offended. In fact, it was painful to hear that something I worked so hard on wasn't received well. When we are only reading words on a screen, we often loose the intention and emotion of the person writing them, so of course, I assumed that he wasn't being nice. I was tempted to jump into the comments and defend myself. Tell him I was just starting out, and that I was doing my best, and who was he to judge me etc. If that is something you do, you aren't alone. A lot of channel owners fall into the habit of rebutting each negative comment. They read negative comments as attacks, worrying that other users will see that, and it will damage their channel.

After I had a moment to think about the comment though, I reconsidered my initial reaction. I imagined the inevitable angry back and forth if I jumped into the fray. I also considered where the poster was coming from. He clearly was interested enough in what I was trying to do in order to sit through my early videos, but he also had more knowledge about audio and visuals than I had, so I decided to engage in a different way. I wrote back, thanking him for the feedback, and I asked for his advice on how I could improve my videos.

On YouTube, or any online message board, this is not the typical way most conversations develop, so initially, the commenter was surprised and probably unsure if I was being sarcastic or not, but through the course of many videos we got to know each other. He provided me with invaluable feedback, until we eventual exchanged phone numbers. He went from our biggest critique to our biggest fan. Whenever I posted a video, he would be the first one to comment. I could always rely on him for genuine feedback as he remained no less picky about my videos than he initially had been. I became just as picky, and my relationship with him catapulted my growth.

I quickly realized from the experience that negative comments provide a great opportunity to learn. When I coach wrestling, I watch the kids closely and when they win, we all celebrate, but when they lose, I ask them what they could have done differently. Those lessons stick with them far longer than the thrill of winning. The same is true of non-positive comments. When you are able to put your ego aside to see the lessons, then you have opened yourself up to grow and improve.

My relationship with the original commenter only improved to the point that my videos eventually surpassed his expectations. He became a fan and supporter of our channel, and I will be meeting him to make a woodworking video with him in the near future. I never delete negative feedback, and I have enough confidence to skip right over the hurt feelings, so whenever I get negative comments, I can immediately turn them into positives for the overall quality of my channel.

As a side note, always try to recognize the difference between trolls and non-positive feedback. Trolls are people who purposefully post negative comments for the sole purpose of getting you to react. They thrive on that negative, argumentative back and forth. You will never sway their opinion and what they have to say will not help you better yourself or your channel. Do not respond to trolls. Do not engage in anyway.

Don't make excuses. Don't become complacent. Listen to negative comments, learn from them and constantly keep growing.

HOW TO USE POSITIVE FEEDBACK

Everyone loves positive feedback, it bolsters your confidence, helps you better handle the negative comments, and signals to other users that your channel has a lot to offer, but as far as providing a lesson for you or your channel, it doesn't help. One key to watch for with positive feedback is the influx of similar positive comments. If on one video, a number of your subscribers, all comment positively on the same thing, maybe it is sound quality or perhaps a particular angle of the camera or a specific explanation, that probably means it was something that you hadn't been doing well in the past, and your audience was just too nice to point it out. Whatever the influx of comments is about, be sure to take note of it and focus on doing it right in your subsequent videos.

YOU HAVE TO ASK

Just because positive feedback is not as rich in lessons, doesn't mean we don't want to continue to encourage positive feedback because positivity is how your community builds. Don't simply expect feedback. You have to ask for it. Many people will watch YouTube to get what they need or want and then move on without ever stopping in the comments section. You have to work at drawing people in enough until they reach the point that they *want* to engage.

This of course begins with quality content that keeps your audience watching, check out Chapter Six and consider how to keep your videos binge worthy. Beyond that, don't hesitate to ask outright for your audience to leave a comment. Including questions in your video is a helpful way to transition into a request to comment. Make sure you time it right and as often as possible keep the questions meaningful, substantive and relevant. Wait to ask until after you have already pulled your audience in with good information. Questions should not just come in the last third of the video after you have already given them tons of free content. Mix it up, keep it fun, we learned by watching other successful channels to ask a "Question of the day." We follow up by repeating "Let us know in the comments below."

We have all seen the videos where the host will ask a light and fluffy question, obviously dropped into videos only to encourage comments so the video will rank up. I have been guilty of asking these kinds of questions from time to time, but I have found that the best kinds of questions are the ones that genuinely require audience feedback. For instance, if I am filming a series of videos, if I ask what the audience wants to see in the next video, the audience feels that their feedback is useful. They will respond, and then they will watch the next video to see if I took their advice. Similarly, I may ask if the technique worked or what challenges the audience faced while doing a project at home. Since, for the most part, the audience wants to follow the video correctly, they will comment with their questions or tips for other viewers.

RESPOND TIME

As you read through this book, you may be getting the sense that everything you do to improve your channel works together. When it works, it acts like well-oiled machine. High quality videos with free, useful information encourage binge watching which can bump you up in the ranks, helping others find you. Responding to comments encourages more engagement which increases viewership etc. But it is your job to keep everything moving. Even shiny new machines need to be maintained. Responding to comments, much like publishing on a schedule or including end screens, is a way to keep your YouTube channel running smoothly.

Once you ask for comments, and your viewers begin to respond, it is then your job keep up your end of the bargain by responding. The time table in which you respond to comments is non-trivial. I mentioned briefly in Chapter Six the importance of responding consistently within the first 24-48 hours. Once you upload a video, stay on top of your comments. When my business consisted of just my wife and I, it could be time consuming and arduous to respond to every comment with genuine responses, but it the long run, it was well worth it. Eventually, as I built a team, I was able to have a dedicated staff just for the comment section in the first two days of uploading a video.

Responding to comments on your own videos increases your visibility, lends you credibility to your audience and of course, further develops your community. This goes back to including your phone number in your videos and developing strong customer service. When your viewers know they can access you with questions and feedback they, simply put, feel good and develop a trust in what you are offering.

The amazing thing that will happen is that your community will become so strong that your long-time supporters and loyal followers will begin to respond for you. If people ask a question, you will see others jump in with the answer before you even have the chance. That doesn't mean that you get to slack off and disappear from the comments, but it does mean you are on the right track.

SUBSCRIBERS VS. ACTIVE USERS

A big part of our goal with engagement is to both attract and encourage more active users, but it is important to note that subscribers and active users are not always the same thing. This can be kind of a catch 22 on YouTube. At the end of each video, we ask users to subscribe, and we often judge a channel's popularity by the number of subscribers. While reminding users to subscribe is important, the underlying goal is active users.

So how then are the two different? Subscribing to your channel means that in that moment, after any particular video, the viewer decided they liked your stuff enough to click subscribe, but that might be as far as their interest in your channel goes. An active user on the other hand is someone who regularly engages with videos by liking and commenting, and they are someone who looks forward to the next video, so when they get an alert on their phone that you have uploaded, they jump right on to watch. Active users are often subscribers, but not all subscribers are active users.

Many times, you find a channel with a massive number of subscribers, but their videos only have a few hundred views and no comments. Often this means that the channel is fulfilling a short-term need. For instance, a channel that teaches its users to do DIY repairs that puts out a few videos on fixing a kitchen sink, will attract users who have an immediate, but short-term need of fixing their kitchen sink. Those users might hit the subscribe button to easily find the channel again while working on their sink repair and watch a handful of videos, but once their sink is fixed, they most likely don't have much need for that channel again until something else breaks in their house. So, while they show up as a subscriber, they are, for the most part, dormant. Keep fixing pain points your subscribers have and watch how your active users will grow!

In my case, these dormant subscribers often are the ones that find me because they are re-doing a countertop in their home. Once the countertop is done, they aren't seeking out my channel any more. The artists, woodworkers, entrepreneurs, and contractors that follow me are a different story. They are the subscribers that can't wait for my next video and will jump right on to comment.

It is my job to show the dormant users what they need along with the other possibilities for my product while also keeping the active users engaged. I aim to meet both types of viewer's needs, however, most of my effort and focus goes toward those reliably active viewers. They are the ones that I can count on, and I want them to be able to count on me and my channel to keep providing what they are looking for. Remember not to get caught up in the subscriber count. Don't compare your channel, improve your channel. At a conference I recently attended for YouTube creators called Vid Summit, I learned a key piece of advice. If you have 1,000 hard core active members of your community who love what you offer, just 1,000 folks who spend $1,000 equals making 1 million on YouTube. Move the numbers around how you see fit but remember active users buy what you recommend because they trust you. You don't need 100,000 subscribers to make a living with YouTube.

I aim to keep the dormant users entertained and interested enough that they don't stop watching just because their short-term need has been fulfilled. It isn't easy to convert a one time or short-term user into an active subscriber. Often, people don't see value in engaging with YouTube channels. They consider videos as a means to and end rather than a way to talk to people or share their opinions. But if you are following the principals of this book, by giving out a ton of great content for free, then they will feel more of a connection and appreciation for what you do. If you ask gently and politely enough, that appreciation can turn an inactive user into an active user.

Use every tool at your disposal to remind viewers about your channel but be careful not to ask for too many actions. If at the end of your video you ask viewers to subscribe, like, share, like on Facebook, follow on twitter and visit your website, they will either get lost in the shuffle or they will be turned off by the demands. Keep it simple, keep it friction free. E-mail marketing can be a great way to gently remind people of new content. Direct people to sign up if they want to hear about future videos, promotions and news within the niche they are interested in. Then once they have signed up, you can send them reminders when a new video is up. The one caveat though is don't abuse the privilege of having access to their email address. If a woodworker signed up, for instance, I wouldn't start sending them emails about art related videos. They would very quickly feel like I had pulled one over on them and would unsubscribe.

In short, don't waste your time soliciting subscribers just to get that number higher. It may look good, but in the end, if no one is actually watching, then that discrepancy can hurt your channel.

MASSIVE ACTION STEP

1. Read your comments

2. Make a list of the most prominent negative comments, what you can learn from them and way to respond positively

Negative Comment	Lesson Learned	Positive Response

3. Use the time table below to create a posting schedule along with a commenting time table.

Video Upload Date	Day One	Day Two

PART FOUR:
FILMING, EDITING AND AUDIO

CHAPTER TEN

The Three Principals of High-Quality Video

Hopefully, by this point in the book, you have a solid understanding of your audience and what philosophies of content and marketing make for a valuable channel, but when all is said and done, the most important thing you need is a good video. You need to make great stuff!

BEGIN WITH THE BEST PART.

For my first video, I got a camcorder and did a shaky cam video from the beginning of a project to the end. It was a single shot with little consideration for the angles or audio. I did no editing before throwing it up on YouTube. Needless to say, it wasn't well received. The few viewers I did get left after the first couple of minutes, and I can't really blame them for that. We have talked before about the goldfish like attention span of most YouTube users. In the first nine seconds of my original video, my viewers were getting me setting up. What are your viewers getting in the first nine seconds of your video? Is it enough to keep them? What is the Hook?

Without knowing what I was even planning on making, no one wanted to suffer through the bad quality of my audio and visual to get to the end. As soon as I started from the "reason to watch", everything changed. If you make only one change to how you present your videos, it should be to begin at the best part of your content. Show them the payoff at the very beginning, so they can decide if your video is something they are interested in.

I started with just a simple shot of the end product edited into the beginning of the video, then I got more sophisticated and started showing a highlight reel including a quick shot of every step they were going to see in the video, prepping, pouring, polishing, the final piece and ending with my logo. All in under 20 seconds. This lets viewers know exactly what they are getting, remember we are telling the truth on YouTube, and it also helps with branding and reliability. As each video starts following the same basic format, viewers know exactly what to expect and can rely on the information they are getting.

Even if you aren't in the do-it-yourself business, every video should start at the wow factor. If you are baking some crazy five tier cake with rainbows and sparkles, no one is going to watch it if you start by putting flour in a mixer without showing them what the end result will be.

HIGHLIGHT REEL

This isn't the first time that I have mentioned the highlight reel, but it is worth spending a little bit of time going over some tips since the highlight reel at the beginning of your video may be what makes or breaks your YouTube viewership.

First, keep the highlight reel brief but informative. When I make highlight reels, I typically keep them between twenty to thirty seconds long. Of course, if your videos are only a couple minutes long, the highlights will be shorter. You want to entice your audience without making them wait too long to get to the real meat of the information.

We will talk about audio in the next chapter, but it is important during your highlight reel that you tell your audience what they are looking at. Playing music is a great way to set the stage and create a feeling, but you want to let people know a few things. 1. How excited you are about the project you are working on. 2. What they are going to learn in the video, and 3. How they are going to learn it. Once again, our goal is to get them excited and interested in what is coming.

With the highlight reel, we aren't forcing the audience to stay to the end to see the finish project, instead we are giving them a reason to want to watch the entire video. The end of the video should have a similar highlight reel. This one can be longer with more shots of the finished product, but once again you should include shots of each step and how you achieved the final result. This is where you can also include a PDF file or any other freebie giveaways you plan on including. If you don't have a physical product you still need to get creative with your highlight reel.

USING YOUR ANGLES

Our original shaky cam videos looked unprofessional to say the least, but that isn't the only reason why you want to up your filming game. Even if you have the best camera that money can buy, using only one camera can really limit your videos. Using multiple cameras makes your videos feel professional, lends you a sense of credibility, and also opens up countless possibilities. In my case, as soon as I got my second camera, my viewership escalated. The more angles you have, the more popular your videos will become. Build a story line with interesting B-Roll shots that entertain and reset interest.

When we only use two cameras, one should remain relatively fixed on the overall wide angle of whatever the main action of your video is, while the other camera moves around getting close ups shots, artistic shots, different participants, this is the B-Roll. Having just one extra camera can change the entire look and feel of your video, giving your audience more of what they want. For example, in my videos, having just a single camera meant that I couldn't always show close up shots of the specific piece of the project I was talking about during any given step, so although I may have been talking about air bubbles or spreading out the epoxy evenly, the audience only got to see it from far away.

As soon as I brought in a second camera, I could start getting those really specific shots. Now during our live videos, we have access to about 25 different angles I can choose from, so if someone steps in front of one shot, we can quickly change to a different angle. I have overhead views, tilted zoom, preset zoom and any other angle that might help me better grab the audience's attention and help them better understand the information I am giving them. To clarify, I don't have twenty-five different cameras, but the software and PTZ cameras we use allows us to seamlessly change angles on individual cameras. Remember, I'm a contractor who knew nothing about making video, but I can learn. (We will cover more about software in Chapter 12: Equipment)

When I went down to Texas to visit Artist Till Death, I brought them an extra camera as a gift, and we set it up in a fixed overhead position. While they were doing their live video, they could switch seamlessly between the front angle shot and the overhead shot allowing their viewers to see exactly what they were doing and the products they were working with throughout the whole video.

Transitioning from a single camera to multiple cameras takes work and planning much like most of the steps in this book, but the payoff in the end is well worth it. I make a habit of watching TV shows similar to what I am trying to do with my channel on the DIY network. My goal is to always duplicate or improve upon what they do. Using multiple cameras is something we see in almost every TV show, but we rarely stop to consider the effect those extra angles have on the production quality of the show. As you watch other channels and TV shows, consider how the added camera's play a role in your engagement, enjoyment and understanding. Take those same ideas and apply them to your own videos. Don't fall into the trap of taking video quality for granted. The quality and production value of your videos make a big impact on how your audience views you. The more angles you have, the more time and effort you will have to put into editing, but in the end, those added angles make your channel look polished and make your videos more enjoyable.

Many channels, not in the do-it-yourself genre, that I call "talking head videos" that rely on a single person simply talking to the camera, may be wondering if this advice applies to them. It does. If you have ever watched this type of video, you probably understand that watching someone speak to you without any thought for the video itself can be boring. By adding interesting or artistic angles, you can provide the viewer with something more engaging. Consider showing video clips of walking through the door, different angles or even filler footage of relevant images that might enhance the overall aesthetic of your video. Your videos only have to be boring if you make them that way. Get creative.

DANGERS OF CLICK BAIT

Just about everyone who runs a YouTube channel wants a lot of video views and a lot of engagement. With this goal in mind, it can become very tempting to fall into the habits of "click bait." Click bait refers to articles and videos on the internet with flashy, alluring titles and images that make big promises about the content contained within, but when clicked on, don't actually deliver on those promises. Click bait is ranked up there as one of the most frustrating and annoying things on the internet right beside pesky trolls leaving nasty comments.

Click bait, at its core is misleading and dishonest. Viewers don't like click bait for two reasons. The first and most obvious, no one likes being manipulated. The second, viewers click on titles and thumbnails that appeal to them. If your video promises to teach them how to increase internet traffic by recreating their whole website in five easy steps, for example, then the viewers genuinely want to learn that. If they click and don't learn that, you have instead taught them that your channel is not helpful and that they cannot trust the content you create.

The rule when it comes to avoiding click bate is simple, treat others how you want to be treated. Your title and thumbnail should reflect what is in your video. You can still optimize it for the algorithm, but don't fall into the trap of using popular keywords just to get people to click. Don't waste their time. It only results in the very audience you are looking to bring in, turning against you in anger.

There is software that I use called "Keywords Everywhere," which we talk in more depth in Chapter 12: Equipment, that allows my team and I to see what terms, phrases and keywords people are searching for. It shows us what is popular, so we can better title our videos. The danger here is using popular, trending terms that don't quite fit your video, but feel close enough that they might work in order to boost your clicks. This is click bait territory. Tread carefully.

This is where bringing in the end results of our content first helps us. Even if we miss the mark on the title, which really shouldn't happen if you are careful, the first thirty seconds clears up exactly what the video holds. There is no danger of click bait if your highlight reel comes first and shows exactly what viewers can expect.

Lastly, if your audience is telling you in the comments that your videos are click bait. Listen. You may not think it is click bait, but that doesn't matter if your audience believes it is. I suspect YouTube's algorithm recognizes click bait, partly through viewer retention statistics. They know when you are tricking your audience or exaggerating with your title and they will punish you for it.

Do yourself, your channel and your viewers a favor by being honest and up front. Provide real content with real value and title it appropriately to continue to build trust and community.

MASSIVE ACTION STEP

1. Using your script from Chapter Six, in the Delivery section, break down the exact components that each of your videos has. For example, mine would be: Materials, Sanding, Mixing, Pouring, Painting, etc. Until we reach the final product.

2. Narrow your list to the top most exciting pieces.

3. Edit those most exciting clips into your highlight reel.

4. How can you use the equipment you have right now to add more angles or include more interesting shots? Make a list of at least four new ideas:

   a. _____

   b. _____

   c. _____

   d. _____

CHAPTER ELEVEN

Audio

The audio quality in your videos matters just as much, if not more, than the quality of the video itself. You can edit out shaky moments or fast forward through dull scenes, but if you don't have good audio, your audience isn't going to stick around. Recently, I met with the crew on the set of American Builder to tape an episode with them. While there, I spent a lot of time with their camera man talking about equipment and audio, and one of the things he said to me was that you can't fix bad audio in post-production, so get it right the first time.

To that end, equipment matters too. We talk at more length in Chapter 12 about equipment, but the most important thing to recognize is that the microphone you are using impacts your audio quality. After talking to the American Builder guys, I bought the same mic they used. It was an expensive investment, but I could certainly notice a huge difference in the audio quality when we switched over. That doesn't mean that you have to drop thousands of dollars up front on a new mic, but you shouldn't rely on the inexpensive or built in camera mic if it's destroying your content value.

VOICE OVER

What happens when you don't get the audio right first time? Early on, I used only native audio, meaning the audio that I recorded while filming my video with either a built-in mic or an external microphone. Relying on only one technique could render entire days' worth of work useless. One time, when I was doing a big elaborate epoxy project with some materials on the more expensive side, I got through three days of shooting with a beautifully finished project, but when I went to edit the video, I realized I had pushed the wrong button, leaving only the audio from my go-pro which was almost entirely unusable.

As my videos got longer and more in-depth it was becoming increasingly difficult to both record perfect video and not shake the flyover shot as I showed the finished product and perfect the audio at the same time. Chances where high that I would either mess up with my audio or make a mistake while filming, and I would have to redo the entire scene from the beginning. In that particular instance, however, I couldn't simply start over. It was a frustrating situation after wasting time, money and beautiful materials, I worried I wouldn't be able to use any of the material that I recorded. After I calmed down, I started figuring out how I could salvage it, and that is when I discovered the power of voice over.

I really fell into voice over accidently and almost reluctantly, but after I used it once, I realized how useful the technique could be. Voice over refers to audio that is recorded after filming is complete and then laid over top of the video in post-production editing. I watched the video that I thought was ruined by bad audio and re-recorded a voice over. The video turned out to be more of a success than I could have hoped for. By making lemonade out of lemons, I learned the benefits of voice over that could be applied to all of my videos at various times. Now when I use B-Roll shots I can piece clips and highlights together while adding a voiceover to bring the attention of my audience to a peak state. It is amazing!

Voice over allowed me to:

1. Talk at normal speeds during a fast forward scene-used to describe what the audience is seeing or talk about what was coming up in the video
2. Re-record your voice to improve imperfections-make sure you say exactly what you want to say without having to remake the entire video scene.
3. Make more entertaining videos-when we change up the audio and narrative it makes our videos more engaging and interesting.

After learning the benefits of voice over through trial and error, we now embrace the new technique and utilize it in almost all of our videos. In the sections of the video that we know are going to be voice over, we are able to film much faster because we don't have to worry about narrating while we work. We have seen an uptick in our audience retention since improving our audio techniques and using voice over.

TALKING ON CAMERA

Talking to a camera is not the same as talking to a friend. I learned this pretty quickly when I started watching the videos I made. You have to learn how to talk to the camera. In addition to the tapes on?? My father also gave me motivational tapes of Zig Ziegler, as a child. At first, he only gave me one tape to see if I would like it. I didn't have high hopes for it, but when I put it on, I realized I was highly entertained, and at the time I couldn't pin point exactly why. I went to my father and asked for the rest of the tapes and proceeded to listen to all of them. At some point during my listening, I realized what it was that entertained me. The information was good, but the thing that really pulled me in and commanded my attention was his voice. He had this way of changing his voice depending on the subject matter. When he was excited, he would speak fast and enthusiastically, and when he really wanted you to listen, his voice would get slow and go down to an almost whisper, until you found yourself hanging on his every word.

That became my model for talking on a camera. I felt really silly at first, talking with more enthusiasm, excitement and inflection than I ever would in my normal life, but if I didn't, it didn't translate onto the screen. In order for the audience to pick up your excitement, you have to multiply it by at least two. My natural voice, tone and inflection all came off as boring, dry and completely unenthusiastic in my videos. If you have the best mic on the planet, it won't make up for your presentation, audio and how you are talking to the camera.

Take the time to learn how to be on camera. Watch people that you enjoy and people that have found success in your niche. Take what they do and integrate what you can into what you do in a way that fits while still being authentic. I am not suggesting that you make up some sort of on-camera persona. Instead, amplify your own personality and strategically incorporate techniques that work until the end result conveys the right amount of energy.

MUSIC

Much like the other audio that you include in your video, music plays a vital role in the overall feel, quality and interest of your video. Changing up the audio can be just as important as changing up the camera angles. Variation of any kind in a video draws the viewers' attention and can help refocus them onto exactly what you want them to see, feel and experience. Think about watching a movie trailer, half of the excitement you feel comes from the dramatic music playing behind the action. The same is true for your videos.

In the beginning I made the mistake of putting a Van Halen song as my intro music. I like Van Halen, and I thought it brought a cool feel to the video, but shortly after, I got a warning that I was using copyrighted material, and the video was blocked. If you use copyrighted music, you can't monetize it, and depending on the copyright protection of the song, the video may be shut down. YouTube Creative Studio provides copyright free music that you can put in your videos for free. The library is extensive with hundreds of artists in all kinds of genres available. We sat down and listened to hundreds of different songs. At the end of the day, we decided that we needed three types of songs; upbeat, dramatic, and suspenseful. We choose about ten songs in each category and started using them across the board. This way, we didn't have to search the entire free music library every time we edited one of our videos, instead we picked from the preselected options.

Having a set playlist of free music also helps with our branding. Our viewers hear a particular song and they automatically associate it with Stone Coat Countertops. They know an exciting part is coming or that a quick over view is coming. We even took the music that plays over our intro and used it as our "hold" music when customers call our phone line. It creates a seamless transition from our YouTube channel to our website, helping customers easily identify with our brand no matter where they go.

MASSIVE ACTION STEPS

1. Spend some time with voice over.
   - ☐ Think about videos that you have made in the past; how would you utilize voice over in those videos?
   - ☐ How can you use voice over moving forward?
   - ☐ Even if your video doesn't lend itself easily to voice over, consider how you can start using it. Are there stock images or videos that you can use to illustrate a point while you are talking?
   - ☐ Study your analytics on videos with voice over. How does the technique improve or change your viewership?

2. Practice talking to a camera
   - ☐ Do a dry run with your script
   - ☐ Film yourself talking and watch it back. Do you sound enthusiastic enough? Does it feel authentic?
   - ☐ Watch others who have found success. What are they doing that you aren't doing? What can you incorporate into your own video?

3. Music: Create at least three categories of music i.e. intro, background, outro or genres of music i.e. upbeat, powerful etc. Then go through YouTube's free music library and make a list of at least ten options.

Music Category	Music Options

CHAPTER TWELVE

Equipment

Building our arsenal of equipment was a long term and ever on-going project for us. We didn't start out knowing what the best equipment was or even having the means to purchase it. Remember, don't let your equipment hold you back from starting. No matter how big, popular or successful your channel gets, there will always be bigger, better, fancier equipment to buy. If you waited until you had only the best equipment, you may never be in a position to get started.

Recognize that your first videos are probably going to be awful. When you look back at them after a year or two you are going to wonder what you were thinking, but as I have said before, you don't know what you don't know. The best you can do is get started and learn as you go. You, of course, need a camera and a mic, but you don't need the top of the line in order to push record and get your channel up and running.

FINDING WHAT WORKS

That being said, it is important to start educating yourself on equipment regardless of where you are in your own growth. The best way to discuss equipment is to share my channel's progression and the differences new equipment made to our channel and the quality of our videos. Like most other small time YouTube channels, we didn't start out knowing everything. While we grew our business and improved our techniques, we also learned about different types of equipment for both audio and video and began incorporating what we learned when it was feasible and appropriate. Much like everything else you will learn in this book, you can't buy success. Rushing out and getting the best camera will mean nothing to your channel if you don't have the education and the skill set to use it yet.

The goal is to get there, eventually, but rushing it may mean you don't get a worthwhile return on your investment. Adapt what you have learned at your own pace in a way that makes sense for your channel's content, budget and growth. Upgrading cameras, mics and software takes more expertise than the lower grade ones require. When you add more angles or more high-tech options you need to know how to use them effectively and that may mean more editing. A lot of YouTube channels out there rely on one cell phone to record their videos, and they have plenty of subscribers. There is no right and wrong, it is simply about what works for your channel. We recently did a collaboration with a channel called Mixed Media Girl. She does all of her videos with cell phone. Her videos turn out great and she has the same number of subscribers that we do. Do what works for you and your audience.

Go back to the chapter on how to listen to feedback and really listen to what they want. When I took the plunge and added a second camera, it was because my audience, in the comments of my videos, were consistently telling me that they wanted up close shots of my project. They wanted to see some of the details I was talking about, and with only one single shot camera that remained relatively stationary on the wide-angle view, I couldn't do that. It became self-evident that it was time to add a camera.

CAMERAS

When we first started our channel, years ago, we used a camera called Flip Share Video. The Flip Share Video was a little mini camcorder, one of the first generations with HD video. Operating it was very simple, straight forward and user friendly. It came with its own editing software that made the videos feel semi-professional for a beginner like me even though the shots and operations were very basic. Only in hindsight did I recognize that it wasn't a very stable camera and the pixels and audio left much to be desired, but at the time, I felt like I was doing a great job. I chose this as my first camera because it was plug and play. I didn't have to know anything about camera, editing or sound to take decent videos right out of the box. They don't sell that exact camera anymore, but it was great for a beginner. When you are starting out, the number one most important quality in any camera you purchase is that you are able to use it. Look for user friendly, plug and play cameras with decent quality. Now a days, technology has improved so much that you can get cameras that do a decent job without breaking the bank. Remember content is always more important than equipment.

When we saw that our channel might actually workout, we started doing some research on what kind of camera to use. We jumped onto YouTube and searched "best ways to make a video." One of the first channels that came up was Sean Cannell of ThinkMedia. He spends a lot of time dissecting the different types of cameras available at a variety of price points. Through watching his videos, we learned how to set up a shot, how to research before recording, and what cameras might work best. We took his advice to heart because he seemed like an honest guy with a straight forward channel.

Armed with some knowledge we purchased our second camera, the Cannon Vixia RF700. It was still a pretty straight forward and simple camera, but the picture quality was better than the Flip Share, so naturally, our videos got better with clearer picture quality. Interestingly, it was the audio that forced us to start researching options to get better close up videos. When the camera zoomed in or out, a slight whirring sound was captured by the mic. I didn't notice the extra sound when I was filming or even editing, although admittedly I wasn't doing much editing at the time, I was simply throwing raw videos up on YouTube, but my audience did notice the sound, and it understandably bothered them. When you are trying to watch a video to learn something new or gain information, you don't want to be distracted by a whirring sound every time the shot zoomed. Rather than venturing into another mic, which I discuss in the Audio section of the chapter, we started looking into cameras that would allow us to zoom. This solved two problems, the first was the annoying sound that zooming caused on our Cannon Vixia and the second was the need to show our projects both up close and in wide shots.

This led us to the GoPro. It was a great upgrade with excellent close up footage and wide-angle shots that showed off the true colors of our products. The GoPro had the added bonus of being small, light and easy to pack if we were shooting in different locations. We ended up getting three GoPros because we liked them so much. One downside of GoPros is that they can over heat very quickly. After about only thirty minutes of filming, they can get over heated and shut down. During our time using GoPros, we experienced lost footage when we ran long and the camera heated up and stopped recording.

Another common complaint about filming with GoPros is the shaky cam effect. It is a real challenge to keep GoPros steady, and if they aren't held perfectly still, you will get shaky, grainy videos. The solution is a tripod or a three-axis gimbal. A tripod, of course, is a basic stand that holds the camera steady in one position and location. A three-axis gimbal on the other hand, is a tripod of sorts that allows you and your camera to move around without the video shifting or tilting. We purchased the Karma Grip, which is a GoPro attachment. You could run with that thing and still get a steady shot without any bounce or shake.

As soon as we switched over to the GoPro and Karma Grip set up, our videos started looking more cinematic. We were able to get really clean, smooth shots of our product and the action of making our counter tops. When we compared the shots from our GoPro to our Cannon Vixia, it made the original footage look awful, so we switched over almost entirely to the GoPro.

We did a lot of videos relying entirely on the GoPro, but as we got more comfortable with making videos, we became dissatisfied with the quality of the GoPro's long shots. Up close and mid-range the GoPro, at that point, couldn't be beat, but when you reached about ten feet away, to get a full shot of me with a finished project for example, the shot suffered. By this point we knew we could do better, so we turned back to researching. We wanted to be careful not to go too big before we were ready for it, so we watched a lot of content that reviewed cameras along with channels that told users what kind of camera they used. I didn't want to fall into the trap of getting a camera that far outpaced my ability to use the hundreds of features and extensive editing options that we didn't know how to use yet. Instead, we went with a Cannon 80D.

I have nothing but great feedback for the Cannon 80D. Part of our decision-making process was determined by filming in other locations. While we have a studio, we wanted to have the freedom to pack it up and go to on-site locations or meet with other channels like Artists Till Death in Texas for a collaboration. In the end, we needed a high-quality camera, that wasn't too overly complex that we needed a degree in cinematography, and it had to be easy to transport. The Cannon 80D fit the bill. We got another three-axis gimbal called the Zhlyun Crane, which works with a DSLR (digital single lens reflex) camera like the Cannon. Once we had the right equipment, we were free to set up one camera on a tripod and another camera on a gimbal that we could carry with us. That way we can get those great stable shots while also getting movement, if we are pouring epoxy or doing other action shots on our project.

Our set up is always evolving as we grow as a channel and as producers. Our current set up consists of one Cannon 80D dedicated to the tripod and another dedicated to the crane. Our goal is to keep getting better. With new experiences and knowledge comes better equipment but be sure that you are comfortable with all of the equipment you have along with the editing requirements before you add to your lineup. We haven't moved passed the auto settings on our latest camera, but with such high-quality equipment, the auto settings work amazingly well with great quality footage, and it gives us the time to learn more in-depth advanced features. The great thing about the Cannon 80D is that is can be a great plug and play and a more advanced camera all in one.

AUDIO

Our progress in audio equipment was not nearly as long or involved as that of our cameras. We used native audio through two cameras. Native audio is the audio taken directly from the mic built into the camera. The Flip Share audio quality was poor to say the least and the Cannon Vixia RF700 wasn't much better. All I had to do was turn slightly away from the camera or walk a couple steps away and the audio quality faded to an almost inaudible quality, and then there was the problem of the loud, distracting zoom. Unbelievably, the GoPro audio was even worse than the native audio in our two previous cameras, and when we attached a gimbal to it, the microphone was covered almost entirely. It was time to finally get an external mic.

Once we transitioned almost exclusively to GoPro, we had no choice but to figure out how to get an external mic. The GoPro requires an attachment in order to connect to a wireless mic. We started with a basic $100 lavaliere wireless mic. The lavaliere mics are wireless mics that clip onto your shirt with a wire that runs down to a battery pack and transmitter that you carry in your pocket, which send the recording wirelessly to the receiver attachment on your GoPro. The mic we choose was the Movow mic 50 from amazon, and it worked out really well. It made a world of difference right away to the quality of our mic, and our audience noticed it too. This allowed us to continue to use the three GoPro cameras we had while patching in the audio into one of them. In editing we could then take any shots we got from the other GoPros and edit them in with the lavaliere mic audio. The audio from the mic was consistent and really helped the quality of our videos. As soon as we switched over, the commenters were commending us for our audio quality.

As we progressed into more advanced cameras with the Cannon 80D, we became dissatisfied with the quality of our mic. When you are first starting out with wireless mics, there is no need to break the bank, but the more we learned the more we wanted the higher quality stuff. After my trip to visit American Builder, their camera man told us about the wireless mic he was using. Since it was always our goal to match or exceed the quality of Television programs, we took the plunge and made the investment on the professional quality stuff. The mic we got was the Sennheiser avx, which cost us about $800, and of course you can't get much better quality. The sound was crystal clear and professional. For my channel, where we were at with our growth and following, it was worth the investment, but again, each channel will have their own natural progression for when it is the right time to drop serious money or just bring in some high quality but less expensive equipment.

LIGHTING

Originally, like most brand-new YouTube channels, we didn't have any extra lighting. In fact, we didn't give much thought to our lighting at all. We had florescent tube lights overhead and if the lights didn't happen to be bright enough or in the right spot for any given shot, the video just suffered. It wasn't until we started reading our comments that we started considering the best way to light our space. We realized again that all of the equipment and software you use works together to create a high-quality video, if any one piece is off, the other equipment can't pick up the slack and make your video better, so lighting is important, especially if the audience wants detailed shots of what you are trying to show them. Low light or deep shadows is going to render your high-def videos useless.

We started with simple umbrella lights that are typically used for photo shoots. These worked great for the most part and some channels may be able to get away with just umbrella lights, but at Stone Coat Countertops, we work with a lot of glossy, highly reflective material, so when we filmed the final product or the high gloss finishes, the umbrella lights lit the room and the participants well, but they created a glare on the epoxy. We added more lights in the corners of our workspace and added de-fusers, which are any devise that spreads out light, in an effort to remediate the glare. After some research and trial and error, we found the best way to reduce the glare was with LED camera lighting.

LED camera lighting allows you to adjust the color from blue to yellow and the brightness and dimness of the light giving you more options within the lighting setup. We decided on the Neewer brand. They are mid-range as far as price and they are high enough quality that they work for us. One important feature for us is their transportability. It is easy to pack them up and bring them with us to different locations.

Spend some time thinking about your lighting. If you aren't ready to make the purchase yet on the lighting, then use what you have. Analyze your space and where the best lighting is coming from. If you have to shoot next to a window or bring in other lights you already own, then do that until you are ready. Do some test shoots to make sure that you have the lighting the way you want it. You don't want to waste time and supplies only to find out later it is unusable.

SOFTWARE

The software you use is important, not because it will necessarily affect your video quality, but because you need to know how to use it effectively and efficiently. As you improve your technology and filming techniques, you are going to find yourself spending more time editing than you had initially. It is important to have software that can keep up with your developing needs without being impossible to use without an advanced degree.

I mentioned that we started out with the software that came with the Flip Share. I graduated to a really easy to use software that came with my computer called Windows Movie Maker. At the time, it was easy enough to use and it had enough features that it was able to meet my needs. Looking back, however, if I only had those two software options to choose from, I would have been seriously handicapped in my editing capabilities.

When I bought my new computer, it no longer came with Windows Movie Maker. At first I was at a loss. I knew the software well, and I worried about learning something new. I spent some time researching and time and again, Adobe Premier Pro came up. I have learned that this is the gold standard of video editing software. People use Adobe Premier to edit anything from YouTube videos all the way up to real movies. Initially it was my intention to purchase Adobe, but my graphics card couldn't handle the power of the program, so I downgraded, in a way, to a program called Filmora.

I consider Filmora to be the idiots guide to film editing. It is user friendly and easy to learn. I got really proficient pretty quickly with it, and as I learned the different features, my videos got much better. I relied on Filmora for about a year without any complaints. Eventually, as my channel got bigger and my editing needs became more extensive, I had to bring a full-time editor on board. When I started interviewing, every single applicant said they had to use Adobe Premier Pro, so I had no choice but to upgrade my computers and implement Adobe. Adobe has a much slower learning curve. It is not nearly as user friendly because it was designed for users who have an education and background in film editing, not for the casual user. I am still not proficient in Adobe, and I imagine it will be some time before I am. When I watch my team edit, it is almost like watching a foreign language.

It you want to start learning the big professional software, then by all means, jump in, but there is nothing wrong with starting at a beginner level and working your way up. The goal is polished professional looking videos, and you should use the software that is the most effective in making that happen.

STAGING

Staging refers to the space in which you are recording your videos. It goes without saying that how you stage your videos is going to be different depending on the content, niche and style of your videos, but as always it is important to carefully consider how your space and staging effect your videos and your audience perceptions. If your space is messy or thrown together, your viewers will see that. They will also judge you for that. Even when we film off sight, we utilize everything available to us to optimize the space, even if it is simply repositioning the people who are going to be on camera to hide a mess or cut out part of the room.

Keep your background flexible, updated and clean. If you do it right, your background can be another tool to brand your videos and encourage binge watching. First, your studio, room, set, or wherever you are filming should be clean. Just like when we talked about your voice inflection being multiplied what it normally would be, the same rule goes for the neatness of your space. In everyday life, having a stack of papers in the corner of your desk is normal, but in your videos, your audience may very likely be distracted by that. Little additions to your space will make a big impact in the look and feel of your video. For example, I added two small lamps to my background set. As far as lighting, they don't do much, but as far as aesthetic, they make my space look more relaxed and authentic. Look at your video through the eyes of your viewer. What is the atmosphere you are creating with your space? If the atmosphere is cluttered, disorganized and poorly thought out, that is what your viewers will associate you, your product and your information with.

Use the background as a way to promote other videos and keep your audience entertained. Your background should not remain stagnant in video after video. Utilize the space to promote your brand. For example, in my studio, we use the wall behind my work space to showcase recently finished projects. The wall is always changing, so it helps to hold the audience's interest. It also acts as instant brand recognition along with the music and logos. The viewers get a quick sense of who we are and what we do simply by looking at the wall behind us, but the most important use for the past projects on the wall is to bring them to other videos. When the audience watches a video and sees something they like on the wall, they will start looking for how to make that. I provide an easy to find link in the description box, and it creates go-to binge watching.

Lastly, consider how you are staging your products. If you are using your products or promoting someone else's, the product label should be on display and easy to read. Product placement should look intentional rather than accidental, as if you forgot about it. Spend time before your video setting up each product that you use. Then, during your video you can discuss each one and go over how you are going to use it

Staging doesn't have to take an enormous amount of effort. It just requires you to put in some conscious thought about what your space looks like from someone on the other end. This applies to every kind of video across the board whether you are a do-it-yourselfer like me or you are a talking head video, backgrounds matter in how the audience perceives you and the value of what you have to offer.

WHAT WORKS AND WHAT DOESN'T

I want to go over a few quick tips and tricks on what works and what doesn't. I don't pretend to have experienced everything, but over time, we have been challenged in unexpected ways, so rather than forcing you to learning through trial and error, here is what I have learned.

- Sound quality of the space you are in is important. In my podcasting space, I hung foam on the walls, so the sound and the noise bounce off really well rather than creating a tinny or echoing sound. We put it up in an interesting geometric way that matches our brand. I was really hesitant about the idea of putting up foam around the whole studio at first, but after listening to the first recording, I realized I didn't have a choice.

- If you film "on location" in really loud spaces, you need a special kind of microphone called a dynamic microphone. The microphones that we use in studio are designed for studio work, and if you used one in a noisy crowded environment, your main dialogue would get lost in the shuffle.

- If you are considering shooting in low light environments, you need to either get another light source or don't do it. In the end, low light makes it difficult to see what you want the audience to see, ending up with really poor-quality footage that will be more frustrating than it is beneficial to your viewers.

- Don't go live in an environment you can't control. Inevitably, murphy's law is going to kick in and something will go wrong, then you don't have the option of editing it out. Your audience may become focused on the things going wrong rather than the point of the video in the first place. Recently, I bought a table at Walmart that we planned on refinishing in a video. I brought the camera along to show where I got the table, how big it was and how much it cost. It was really interesting content, but It wasn't enough to make a whole video. Instead, we patched it in throughout the shots of the project. Filming in public places can get tricky. You want to control as much as you can. Often these big businesses don't appreciate when you go in there with all your big camera equipment. Instead, I opt for some cell phone footage or a more low-key camera. The video quality may not be the best, but you work with whatever you can.

- When you start utilizing a team to help with editing or camera work like I eventually did, make sure that they are a part of every step along the way. If you have them just jump in on a camera every once in a while, you are going to get frustrated because they don't know all the ins and outs of the company. Each step of planning, set-up, recording, editing, uploading and cleanup of a video is connected, and your employees and collaborators should be tuned into that.

- We always have a checklist whenever we are filming. Inevitably, you are going to make a lot of mistakes, when mistakes come up, add it to the checklist. Then the next time you are filming, go through that checklist. Make sure there are batteries in the camera, make sure the mics are turned on and charged. A survivalist buddy of mine always said, "one is none and two is one," so when I get on a plane to meet with a collaborator, I always make sure I have backups.

GOING LIVE

Going live is its own category when it comes to equipment, software and strategy. Everything I learned leading up to going live had to be re-written, re-examined and re-formulated for our live videos. The benefits of the live videos are amazing, but it takes a lot of planning to hit the ground running with the live videos.

Doing live videos is not user friendly with any of the equipment we currently had. We couldn't simply plug in the camera equipment into our computer and live stream it. We needed to get video capture devices and software that makes that equipment work.

We started by taking a class from Sunny Lenarduzzi, who I have mentioned previously. She suggested a software called Open Broadcaster Software (OBS). OBS is a free, open share software that allowed us to capture live streams from many different devices, cameras and audio sources and bring them all into one application on the computer. That way, we could still utilize the technique of multiple shots during the live feed. Once all of the devices are brought into the software, it allows you to switch your live feed from camera to camera. It even allows you to share what is on your screen and other media.

From there we had to find the right camera. We found that web cameras were the most well suited for live feeds. Just like the other cameras we used for our regular videos, we learned not all cameras are created equal. We eventually settled on the Logitech C920. A lot of people had recommended the camera for YouTube live stream. We started out with just one to try it out, but then we broadened out to two, then three until eventually we had six cameras up all over the studio. Unlike the cameras we use for regular videos, the Logitech cannot be preprogramed with multiple angles, so we needed more physical cameras around the studio.

An important note to mention is that if you are pulling up multiple shots from multiple feeds during your live stream with the OBS then someone needs to be stationed at the computer throughout the entire video pulling up the shots when they are needed. It is not like during our regular videos, in which we pull from different cameras and angles in post-production. Having someone at the computer also means they can keep an eye on the live comments, so if your viewers want to see something again or a different shot, you can respond to it instantly, which is one of the greatest benefits of live streaming. The final step was brining it all together. In a live video, it is still important to include branding, intros, and some music to keep it interesting.

It was not an easy process. Initially, I was reluctant to even jump into the live video arena because it presented a lot of challenges. When you are working on a do-it-yourself project, a lot can go wrong. The audience gets to see every mistake you make, but they also get to see every victory too. We realized that being able to have an almost instant dialogue with our audience really increased the engagement. They could give their input while also getting a real sense for how long projects take, how easy it is, and how to fix mistakes on the fly. I learned that just because something is challenging doesn't mean it isn't worth doing.

The more comfortable we got with live streaming the more we wanted to improve. It was the same sentiment we had with our regular videos. The C920 cameras were a decent starter camera, but we wanted to get even better, clearer shots, so after some research we decided on a Point Tilt Zoom Camera. They were basically designed as security cameras or for web conferencing in which you could easily move the camera and refocus it on something else, including small handwriting all the way across the room. This camera created amazingly detailed zooms and also allowed us to preset some different zooms, so we could just hit a button and it would automatically move to a different location and a different zoom. Our live stream computer guy, who happened to be my brother, could then transition between shots efficiently and seamlessly. The Point Tilt Zoom we chose was the Aver Cam520. It was about eight times the price of the Logitech, but it was also eight times better. When we got one of the AverCam520s our Logitechs looked pretty low quality in comparison, so we had to, over time, replace each Logitech.

We have found great success with live streaming, but don't rush it. With other videos, my advice is "Go! Get started!" with live videos, my advice is making sure you have the minimum equipment, software and planning to do a good job. You don't want your live streams to look low quality in comparison to your regular videos. Again, that doesn't mean you need the most expensive equipment, but you do need a plan.

***

When guests entered our studio, they were blown away by the professionalism of all the equipment. It had really come a long way since the very beginning with the one little Flip Share Video. The transformation didn't happen overnight, instead, it happened over years. I started out filming my construction work and trying to sell my product with before and after pictures, but a video would be worth a million words rather than a thousand.

Expensive equipment is not necessary. You should still follow the advice from the first few chapter of this book-get started! But as you grow, let your equipment, software, and studio grow with you. Try better mics and cameras within your budget. Do your homework, research, plan and experiment with different ideas and techniques.

MASSIVE ACTION STEP

- ☐ What equipment do you have right now that will help you press record?

- ☐ Make a "wish list" of equipment. Include what steps you need to take in order to reach those goals.

Equipment	Steps to Take	Timeline

PART FIVE:
BRINGING IT ALL TOGETHER

CHAPTER THIRTEEN

Broadening Your Horizons

Throughout this book, we have discussed a lot of short term and longer-term fixes that will improve your videos and your reach, but it is important to think about your long-term goals as well. When you first picked up this book, your goals may have been to simply increase subscribers or improve the audio and visual quality of your uploads, but now that you are on your way to reaching those initial goals, it is time to create more goals. Those goals should include broadening your horizons and giving back to the community you are a part of.

EXPANDING YOUR REACH WITH SOCIAL MEDIA

The first step in broadening your horizons involves branching out on social media. We spoke briefly about this when we went over your marketing funnel, but I want to go into a little more depth here because now that you have your YouTube channel (mostly) in order, it is the time to start putting some thought into expanding out. This of course helps your marketing funnel. A lot of people stick mainly to one form of social media, so if you are only focusing your efforts on YouTube, you are missing out on opportunities to reach an audience that may be interested but unable to find you. Beyond simply bringing potential clients and viewers to your channel, you can also create new ways for users to connect meaningfully to the community you are trying to create.

Facebook

I branched out into Facebook Groups, a very powerful social media option, very reluctantly after some coaching from Sunny Lenarduzzi, but rather than start a Facebook page or a personal page, she suggested we start a Facebook group. That was some of the best advice I have received around the use of social media. Facebook, a while back, changed their algorithms to strongly encourage, or even force, users to pay for ads. What that meant was when you publish a post on your Facebook page, very few people were going to see it. Even friends and people who have "liked" your page were unlikely to see your posts, so pages and people who built a huge following were now virtually invisible.

Facebook then suggests you create an ad to boost your post and extend your reach. This is something we do. We do run Facebook ad campaigns. Essentially you pay Facebook to put your content in front of not only your existing followers but potential customers as well. Facebook ads work in a similar way to Google and YouTube ads. You essentially create a target audience for your ads that can include a huge number of attributes including interests, home owner status, income, location, other liked pages and so on. From there you set a goal of either link clicks, likes, comments, video views or other interactions. Once it is set up, you set a daily budget and let Facebook do its magic. These ads have worked really well for us because our audience is specific and targeted. Like YouTube, the people who interact with your ad end up, more often than not, turning into customers because you have already guaranteed they have a high interest in what you are doing through the way you target them, so for very little money you get a lot of people visiting your YouTube or your website. If you are selling something like sunglasses, you may have a harder time narrowing your audience enough. If you don't narrow your audience enough, your ad is too broad to have a worthwhile return on investment. You may end up throwing money at an ad to reach people who have no interest in buying your product. In short, the key to Facebook ads is your audience. Go back to chapter two and revisit tips for knowing your audience before you start entering criteria for your Facebook ad.

Facebook groups, on the other hand, allow you to reach an audience without dropping any money at all. A Facebook group is not a business page or personal account, but rather a virtual gathering place of likeminded individuals. That means your posts and the posts of members are not filtered through an algorithm like they are on other types of pages. We set up a group for do-it-yourselfers, that are using our product, to get together. They discuss their projects, ask questions, share videos etc. in a natural and organic way. At first, I was concerned about the relative lack of control that a group presents. Would we get naysayers or big complainers? Would we get enough people interacting? But in the end, it turned into a huge success. In about six weeks the group grew to about six thousand members. So, when we post something to the group it reaches six thousand people instantaneously. We use it as a type of beta testing for different ideas. We will put up polls asking them what they think of different ideas. They start to feel like part of our "tribe" to the point that they really value their place in the community.

LinkedIn

LinkedIn is an interesting social media platform that has not grown and evolved in the same way Instagram, Twitter, and Facebook have. When Microsoft bought it recently, they revamped the entire system leaving it open to potential. Since it is still young and often over looked, it leaves a lot of potential for organic business to business content. So, we use it to share a lot of raw form content directed at business owners. For example, we plan on putting up a video on how to remodel a restaurant on a budget. That is something that restaurant owners are searching for and they can find it right on LinkedIn. We also will share content on how to train employees or how to keep your team happy. LinkedIn is a great place to test out new content and broaden your reach specifically to other businesses.

Instagram, Snapchat & Pinterest

Instagram is great for short form content. We use it to post quick snapshots of our videos that in turn lead users back to YouTube. It is also great for pictures of finished projects that work to intrigue potential clients and again lead them back to YouTube. As a community in and of itself, it isn't as robust as Facebook and doesn't provide as much of a new audience as LinkedIn. But we have found that people enjoy seeing the pictures and videos.

The other social media: Pinterest, Snapchat and Tumblr, don't take up a lot of our time or focus. We will update those pages periodically, but the main goal, like Instagram is to draw people toward our videos.

Amazon

Beyond social media, Amazon offers what is called affiliate marketing. Depending on how you implement it, it can either be extremely powerful or extremely damaging to your brand, so use it wisely. Essentially, Amazon's affiliate program allows you to earn money through marketing other people's products. For example, at Stone Coat Countertops, we use the same torch every day when we are working on an epoxy product. The torch sells for about $36 to $40 depending on the exact torch you are going to get. On my channel, we talk about the torch, explaining why it is our favorite one to use, but I don't want to take on the responsibility or added expense of shipping, stocking and selling them. And more likely than not, I couldn't make a profit unless I was charging more than you could get them for at Home Depot or Amazon. Instead, it is a great product to be an affiliate marketer for. I know it is a great product, and I already talk about them on my channel, so it is easy to point my viewers to a link where they can purchase them on Amazon.

I created a section on my website called "Our Favorite Tools" that is a list with names and links to the tools we use in our videos. My viewers for the most part find this very helpful because it is another friction free path to get the tools that I am using. Each time someone follows our link to purchase that product we get some small portion of the sales.

There are a few caveats with this. The first, always tell your audience. Be honest with them that you are getting a kickback when they are buying the tool, but that it doesn't cost them anymore and really helps out your channel. The second caveat is that you have to be genuine. If you are lying about a product just so you can get a kickback, your audience is going to find that out fast, and they are not going to be happy. Make sure that you believe in the products that you are putting your name behind otherwise people will lose trust in your word and your brand. Tell the truth.

Just like with the money I get from monetizing my videos, I don't rush out to buy a new car or take a vacation, instead I put that money right back into my business. I use it for new equipment, more advertising or even just basic office supplies.

The great thing about affiliate advertising is that it doesn't cost me a thing, and the company that advertises with me only pays for a sale, which in most other types of marketing is unheard of. Even in Google and YouTube you are paying for a potential sale, but in affiliate advertising the company only pays when someone makes a purchase. It is a win-win situation because my audience is getting a direct, easy to use link to a product they want, I am getting money that I can put back into my business, and the manufacturer is paying only for sales.

Shipping

Shipping is an important aspect of any business that deals in physical products for purchase. This will not apply to every business model, but it is important to establish strong shipping practices right away. First, always remember that your biggest competition is Amazon. If you aren't shipping in two or three days, you better figure out how to make that happen. If your customer is ready to buy, and they see that your shipping takes a week or more, they are likely to pull up amazon and start comparison shopping. The key to fast shipping is investing in your inventory, quality, and training. Keep your inventory high, train your staff well and make sure the quality is there. Every box gets packaged in exactly the same way, turning our shipping department into almost an assembly line. Everything is done exactly the same way each time, so it becomes predictable, fast and easy.

We view shipping as just another step in our marketing funnel because we don't want anyone to be disappointed in our products. When they open that box, we want it to be an exciting experience. We include thank you notes along with directions on how to leave a review if they are so inclined. Take the time to plan your shipping strategies before your first box ever goes out to ensure that the positive feelings you created leading up to the purchase continue all the way through to final use.

CREATING CONNECTIONS

Creating connections to other YouTubers and industry leaders has made a nearly immeasurable impact on our growth. We would not be where we are today without our connections to what we call influencers. Influencers don't have to have a huge following. Sometimes influencers have a smaller audience, but what you really want to look for are people who really relate to your channel, who can provide you with great, helpful information, or who may open up more doors for you. For example, as a DIY channel, we wouldn't benefit from connecting with political YouTubers. Those topics don't relate to what we are doing and might even turn people off. Instead we have sought out other DIY channels and channels in more creative fields. We have had some amazing experiences working with other channels.

The benefits of creating connection with other influencers are of course increased viewership on your own channel, but we have also learned so much and met some great friends and colleagues along the way.

Whenever we fly out to meet someone, or have them fly to us for a collaboration, whatever we have spent on airfare, hotel, car rentals, products, shipping, you name it, it has been well worth the expense for the connections, relationships and ultimately the sales that came about.

Paul's Toolbox

One of our first collaborations was with Paul Richdale, a firefighter out of Louisiana. He wanted to learn how to use some of our products on a project he was doing. At the time I only had about 5,000 subscribers while he had well over 100,000. When he reached out to me, I was extremely flattered. He liked how I came off on camera, and he took me under his wing, mentoring me and helping me out. From the moment we met, we made a mutual connection, and to this day, we have each other on speed dial. He never asked for anything in return. He simply wanted to help. That type of connection is rare and probably doesn't happen all too often, but when it does, treat that person with your utmost gratitude and pay it forward. Make sure that it is a win-win situation and that you do everything you can to repay that generosity.

See Jane Drill

Leah from the YouTube channel See Jane Drill reached out to us because she liked our product. She thought doing a video with us and our product would be a great program for their channel. Again, at the time, we didn't have many subscribers yet, but See Jane Drill had about a quarter million subscribers. They drove out to our little shop from Seattle. During her visit, I learned so much from her. She had been to VidCon, a big YouTube creator summit, and she shared a lot of tips and tricks that helped jump start our success.

American Builder

I have mentioned Brian Gurry from the TV show American Builder before in the book. He had a lot of experience and even won some Emmys for his work. He of course provided me with a lot of insight into equipment and video editing. My collaboration with him changed the way that we filmed our videos and pushed us to make bigger and better goals for our channel. Rather than simply getting more subscribers, I set out to be better than DIY TV. We knew that with enough practice we could achieve that goal.

Carl Jacobson

Carl Jacobson has over 200,000 subscribers on his woodworking and wood turning channel. With Carl, we ended up reaching out to him because one of our team members at Stone Coat headquarters came across the channel and realized he was in Oregon, so we asked him if he would like to team up. He drove out to our shop with his trailer, and we made a piece for his mobile shop. He was such a nice guy and so grateful. In the end we shared content, made a great product, and it was a win-win.

Oregon Burls

Greg, The Burl Hunter, only lives about ten miles from us, and he had been on National Geographic and a show called Filthy Riches. Greg didn't have a lot of influence at the time. When he first started out on YouTube, he gained a following, but after he moved over to TV, his YouTube channel lost its influence. When he reached out to me, his goal was to rebuild his YouTube following because he recognized how powerful YouTube had become. It was interesting when he reached out because he wanted to know who was making our videos, so he could hire them too. When I told him that I was the one doing the editing, he was surprised and impressed. That was one of the best compliments I have ever received. From there, we did a collaborative video in which he gave us a burl, which turned out to be one of our most successful videos. He came to our studio, and I showed him everything I was doing with editing. I also visited his studio to get a feel for the kinds of stuff he was doing.

Greg and I became fast friends. I showed him everything I knew about shooting better video, and I introduced him to my audience because his burls and raw wood were exactly the kinds of things my audience was interested in. A big key that you can gain from collaboration is getting out of your environments. Show off other people's sets, studios and workspaces. Heighten interest in your videos by going to new place. Give your audience something fresh, new and genuine.

Artists Til Death

I have mentioned Artists Till Death previously in the book, but I cannot overstate how helpful and mutually supportive that connection has been. Artist Till Death are a team of two people, Erica and Jeff. They had a relatively small audience compared to my channel, but they used my products in a way that I hadn't thought of before. I do a lot of various art projects and push the envelope, but at the time I began our collaboration, I stuck to woodworking and DIY home projects. When Erica and Jeff contacted me, they told me how much they liked my products and suggested filming a test. They warned me ahead of time that it would be an honest test. That was a gamble. If they hated it then that video might turn some of my customers off, but I believed in my products and sent them off to be tested. Of course, much to my relief, they loved our products.

After that, we offered them a sponsorship. Anytime they used our products, we would pay for them, giving it to them for free in order to show case it in their videos. We agreed that if there was anything they weren't one hundred percent happy with, they would be honest with us, and we would work with them to replace it. That began an amazing, open, honest relationship, and the benefit of which lends great credibility to our products. They benefit from the free materials for their videos, and we benefit from honest reviews that potential buyers can see. Our relationship with Artists Till Death, also led to many other relationships with artists on YouTube including Marcy from Mixed Media Girl, who came from LA to do a collaboration, and Christina Welch who works a lot with acrylics but now loves our epoxy.

***

In only about a year and a half time frame, we developed many strong, mutually beneficial relationships simply by reaching out and offering whatever help we had to offer. We also, of course, reached out to channels that weren't like our own but might offer the opportunity to learn more about YouTube and marketing, such as Sunny Lenarduzzi and Gary Vee. Not everyone you reach out to will be receptive. Some people many not even respond, but you miss 100% of the shots you don't take, so take the chances.

MASSIVE ACTION STEP

- ☐ Create accounts on at least two new social media platforms
- ☐ For each day on the schedule below, write which social media you will post to, and what you will post.

Sun.	Mon.	Tues.	Wed.	Thur.	Fri.	Sat.
Ex. Facebook highlight reel from most recent vid.						

☐ Research potential amazon affiliates

☐ Use the table below to better understand your current shipping practices and what you would like them to be.

	Current Practices	Goal	Steps to Get There
How long does it take to get a package ready to ship?			
After Packaged, how long does it take to get out to the mail?			
After it is mailed, how long does it take to get a customer?			
What do packages look like?			
What extras are put in packages?			
How do you thank customers?			
What follow up do you do?			

CHAPTER FOURTEEN

Final Thoughts

LEARN TO DO IT YOURSELF

I always tell people to learn to do things yourself, and I have found that it is a hotly debated piece of advice. Some people will adamantly argue that you should seek out and hire experts first, but I want to explain why I believe in doing it yourself first.

In building my business, I did a lot of things wrong, but I also did a lot of things right. Along the way one of the things I learned was that if I can learn everything I can about a topic myself then I will have a clear handle on my business. In the beginning, I didn't have a choice. I didn't have the money to hire someone to build a website, run our ads or edit our videos. I couldn't even hire employees to pack my boxes, so instead I let my kids help out in the beginning. I was forced to learn from scratch. I watched other people's videos, read articles and did what I had to do to keep moving forward. I learned about advertising, thumbnails, digital media, shipping, computers, you name it, and I had to learn it.

It was hard work, but because I learned all of these lessons, I was able to know exactly what I wanted my company to look like, and when it came time to start hiring, I could find the right people and communicate what I wanted without the risk of them trying to pull one over on me. Further, many workers for hire in the various industries needed to run a YouTube channel and a business will not be connected to your content or products in the least. At one point we tried to outsource our marketing to a company, but in the end, they were completely disconnected from our product, our audience and our goals as a business. It was nearly impossible to convey exactly what we were looking for, and more often than not, larger companies follow basic routine formulas in a one size fit all approach that probably don't actually fit your business. No one, not even leading experts, will be as invested in your business as you are. Build the foundation of each aspect of your business yourself before you try to bring in help, otherwise, your business will be shaped by their philosophies, practices and visions rather than your own because you will have no choice but to trust in what they are doing.

Eventually you will hire a team, but if I didn't know how to do these things myself, I wouldn't even know what to ask of my team. It is my job to lead and guide them. Without a basic understanding of the ins and outs of my own company, I can't possibly be a strong leader.

Without the experience of logging hours studying my analytics, editing videos, and adding keywords to my ad, I wouldn't have been able to tell my in-house editors to add a hook to the front or fast forward through the sanding or add a voice over as I pour. I found my creative voice through learning everything myself. Doing it yourself puts you in the driver's seat. It brings you closer to your audience, your product and your videos.

Being in the driver's seat of my own channel and business also helped me develop processes. Processes are key to scaling your business as you grow. I developed a process for every aspect of my channel and business from editing, to customer calls, to shipping. Each process was clear, so that others could step in and continue the work without changing the fundamentals of the business. From the process came the absolutes. The absolutes were the way we did things in any given situation in a definitive way for the team. Brand new situations come up every day, making the absolutes a living document. We have trained our team on how to write an absolute, so that everyone can contribute, but they can't take away without approval from a manager. This allows us to implement changes quickly and effectively.

BUILD AN AMAZING TEAM

That brings us to hiring your team. When your company grows big enough that you can't possibly do everything yourself, you will start hiring. Building a team, in my opinion, is always a better option than outsourcing. My original team consisted of myself, my wife, my three oldest boys, even our baby would encourage us by cheering us along. As a family we worked really hard. We made a goal of paying off our house together to get out from under that debt. It is a modest house, living well within our means, so it was a goal we thought we could achieve, and we did. After our first year, we paid off the house together. But then it was time to hire a team. By that point the channel and business had grown to the point that my first team, my family, was drowning. My wife and I would stay up until three in the morning working on videos, answering comments and preparing shipments.

So, my first hire was my father. At the time, he needed a job. My whole life he had taken care of me, even getting me a job and teaching me everything I knew about construction, so this was a great opportunity to pay it forward to him. He became our shipping manager. From there I hired my brother to be the customer service manager. Then we started hiring close friends. Eventually, we grew big enough that we needed to put an ad out on Craig's list. After having done the leg work to build the company myself, I knew exactly what I needed in an employee and was able to put out the ad and interview with that knowledge in mind. We were able to build a solid, reliable team that was more like family than simply a group of employees. The best part about bringing them all together was the relationships we built together. We have a common goal and the processes in place to really succeed.

An important lesson that I learned through the process was to be willing to let people go when it just wasn't the right fit. This was a hard lesson for me to accept, but if you keep people on your team who don't fit, in order to spare their feelings, the end result is worse than the initial sting of letting them go. I find that while onboarding new employees is important, "out" boarding them is even more important. When an employee isn't the right fit, we give them as much help as we can set up. We give them feedback that will help them for their future and set them up with recommendations whenever possible.

Our team is so important to us. Taking care of your team and making sure they are happy, creates a successful business. Without our team our business wouldn't be successful, so it is important to hire qualified, like-minded team members and to take the time to train them and provide the support they need.

TAKE THE BLAME

I learned early on from Gary Vee that everything is my fault, and it changed my whole mind set. If you are running a business or a channel, it is important to take full responsibility for it. When you take responsibility for everything that goes wrong within your business, you can spend more time focused on how to fix it rather than on who to blame or what went wrong. When something goes wrong, I think: I didn't train someone well enough, I didn't have the right process in place, or I didn't foresee this problem.

On YouTube, you need to say everything that needs to be said and not one thing more. The same is true in business, you need to have every process that needs to be in place, but not one process more. Don't over complicate things. Don't bog down your team unnecessarily with needless checks and balances that will slow things down and create friction. Trust that they can handle things, and when things go wrong, focus on the fix.

The plus side of taking all the blame when things go wrong is that you also get to take on some of the accolades when things go right. I get to acknowledge that when it worked, it worked because of all the hard work that we put in. I started out as a contractor who knew nothing about this stuff, but I took on the responsibility and worked hard through trial and error and eventually found my way to success.

FOLLOW WHAT WORKS

There are no hard and fast rules in YouTube. The platform and users are changing so quickly that if you simply apply the advice from this book and then don't change a thing, you may not see the results you had been hoping for. It is important to follow what works for you and your channel. The advice you get from this book, or any other source, is simply a starting point for your own personal journey. Don't discount your knowledge, experience and intuition. If something works for you. Do it. If something doesn't work for you. Change it.

That being said, don't spread yourself too thin. This especially applies to social media. If you are trying to keep up with six or seven social media sites, YouTube and your website, you will inevitably start dropping the ball and your content and customer service will suffer as a result. We make a schedule and divide up our content throughout but keep our focus on what has been proven to work.

As a team, we have clearly delineated priorities of who and what gets first dibs on our attention. First priority is in person customers who walk through our door. If someone walks into our building, team members know to drop everything and attend to them. The second priority is answering phone calls. In the age of technology and online communication, when a customer takes the time to pick up the phone and talk directly to us, we have found their commitment to our company and products is already pretty high, and it is important to meet their needs promptly. The third priority is responding timely to emails. The fourth priority is responding to comments on social media. We break this fourth priority up even further with YouTube comments getting top billing followed by Facebook, then by all the other social media. Our team members understand the priorities, and this helps prevent anyone person from falling down a rabbit hole of comments or spreading themselves too thin.

Not spreading yourself too thin applies to implementing changes as well. Whenever you are preparing to try something new, it is important not to try everything at once. If you take all the advice from this book and try to implement it all at once, getting new camera, renaming videos, updating your thumbnails etc. And all of a sudden, your video views and subscriptions take off, you won't know what to give credit to. You also run the risk of overwhelming yourself and burning out.

The best way to move forward is to start by making small measurable changes, watch your feedback and analytics to see what effect the changes had before moving on to make more. For example,

I just did a series of four videos with Marcy from Mixed Media Girl and put them all up right in a row because my art videos were doing really well, but when the series finished, and I posted a countertop video, I got a lot of comments saying something to the effect of, "hey we are really glad you did some countertops again." Essentially, a large portion of my audience liked the art, but they were really there for the countertops. Instead of putting up all the new art videos in one go, I should have spread those out. The same is true of your changes. If you change too quickly you may lose your base audience or change something that shouldn't be changed. Unless you are moving slowly enough, you may not even understand why.

You are going to grow exponentially as you begin following the advice in this book. You will find new areas to do videos on, bring in other collaborators, improve your filming, editing and sound techniques as well as your marketing. All of this will expand your reach and grow your channel, but don't lose yourself in it. Remember this book is How I Made a Million by Telling the *Truth* on YouTube. That truth part is the most important part. Remain genuine. Do what works for you rather than trying to become someone or something else. When you follow what works for you, your content and channel will remain genuine and honest.

Recently we hit 100,000 thousand subscribers, and we got a letter and our YouTube silver play button. I read the letter out loud on a live stream, and one of the lines in the letter said, "A million subscribers is much closer than you really think." That line stuck with me because it had never crossed my mind to have a goal of a million subscribers, but it's true. Whatever your goal may be, it is closer than you think. Get excited about the future and get to work.

Congratulations on taking this first step!

Remember, until next time from Mike Quist,

You Got This! I'll see you on the next video.

ABOUT US

I know this book will find its way into the hands of folks who are looking to make a difference in their lives and the lives of others. With encouragement I want you to understand and believe you can do it! In 2008 my wife and I lost our home, we almost lost one of our son's, and I almost died from a construction injury. Our lives were upside down. We took all the resources we had and moved our lives to a piece of raw land in the woods in Oregon. We had no running water, we fixed up a small travel trailer, and we simply started from square one and pressed go. We built our home from the ground up, little by little as we could afford to. We built our shop little by little, and we built our business. I believe it is possible to use You Tube to get your message heard. If I could do, it so can you. I want to sincerely thank My beautiful wife Kathryn for always saying yes and believing in me. I thank my sons who will follow me into battle with out second thought. I thank my Mom and Dad for the belief they have in me and the priceless lessons they imparted to me in my life. I want to thank my brother for his belief in me and our business. I thank my team and their amazing love. I thank those who have collaborated with us. I thank our subscribers from the bottom of my heart. I thank my Father in Heaven for the life I have. I want to thank you for reading this book.

RESOURCES

For more resources and links to all of the equipment, software, tools, resources and pages mentioned in this book, visit www.StoneCoatCountertops.com

Made in the USA
Columbia, SC
09 December 2018